Some Useful Wild Plants

Some Useful
WILD PLANTS

A Foraging Guide to
Food and Medicine from Nature

Revised Edition

DAN JASON
Illustrations by Robert Inwood

**HARBOUR
PUBLISHING**

Harbour Publishing Co. Ltd.
P.O. Box 219, Madeira Park, BC, VON 2H0
www.harbourpublishing.com

Indexed by Tori Hannesson
Cover illustration by Robert Inwood
Text design by Brianna Cerkiewicz
Printed and bound in Canada
Printed on FSC-certified, chlorine-free paper made from 100% post-consumer fibre

Plants have distinct effects on different people. It is vital that you consult your health care provider before considering any self-directed treatment of a medical condition, including the use of wild food and medicinal plants. Be vigilant when consuming wild plants: if you notice any negative effects, discontinue use and consult your health care provider immediately. Some beneficial plants closely resemble other plants that are toxic to humans. Before you consume any wild plant, consult with an expert to be certain that you have correctly identified it.

Harbour Publishing Co. Ltd. acknowledges the support of the Canada Council for the Arts, which last year invested $153 million to bring the arts to Canadians throughout the country. We also gratefully acknowledge financial support from the Government of Canada through the Canada Book Fund and from the Province of British Columbia through the BC Arts Council and the Book Publishing Tax Credit.

LIBRARY AND ARCHIVES CANADA CATALOGUING IN PUBLICATION

Jason, Dan, author
      Some useful wild plants : a foraging guide to food and medicine from nature / Dan Jason ; illustrations by Robert Inwood. -- Revised edition.

Includes index.
Previously published: Vancouver : Talonbooks, 1972.
Author of original edition: David Manning.
Issued in print and electronic formats.
ISBN 978-1-55017-791-6 (softcover).--ISBN 978-1-55017-792-3 (HTML)

      1. Wild plants, Edible--British Columbia--Identification. 2. Wild plants, Edible--Northwestern States--Identification. 3. Medicinal plants--British Columbia--Identification. 4. Medicinal plants--Northwestern States--Identification. 5. Cooking (Wild foods)--British Columbia. 6. Cooking (Wild foods)--Northwestern States. 7. Indians of North America--Medicine--British Columbia. 8. Indians of North America--Medicine--Northwestern States. I. Inwood, Bob, illustrator II. Title.

QK99.M3 2017   581.6'30971   C2016-907689-X
                                           C2016-907690-3

Contents

Introduction

I'm very happy to be writing this new introduction to *Some Useful Wild Plants*, which was first published over 45 years ago, in 1971!

When I came out to British Columbia after graduating from McGill University in 1967, one of my first new friends was David Manning. (We're still great buddies nearly 50 years later!) Even though my degree was in psychology and anthropology, I had a love for plants in my blood and bones. David stoked my desire to learn more about plants because of his great familiarity with all things that grew in the wild.

There weren't many books on foraging for wild plants back then, and we got the idea to write a really good, all-inclusive one. With support and encouragement from Tom Perry, Nancy Cundill and Gregg Macdonald, I ended up being the main researcher and writer. I interviewed First Nations herbalists and Doukhobor wild-crafters, spent lots of time in libraries and trekked all over southern BC, eventually finding all the plants I was looking for.

We convinced our good friend Bob Inwood to do the illustrations, and I still have fond memories of taking Bob into forest and field to capture the plants with his beautiful line drawings. I am grateful to Bob for allowing a new generation of plant lovers to see his fine renditions.

At that time, we were based in the Slocan Valley in the

BC Interior and the first edition of *Some Useful Wild Plants* focused on plants that were found there. When David and I took our manuscript to David Robinson of Talonbooks in Vancouver, he was immediately very enthusiastic. Before long, I was taking copies to bookstores across southern BC.

There was such a great demand for our book that we soon created an expanded version that was relevant to all of British Columbia. In fact, most of the wild plants in this book are found across North America. *Some Useful Wild Plants* became a bestseller that was reprinted six times. I saw copies everywhere I went. I felt so gratified that I had helped initiate a revival in the appreciation and utilization of wild plants that could be found in city and country, field and forest, garden and farm.

Many glossy books on edible and medicinal wild plants have come out since then, but I still delight in Bob's illustrations and feel good about what I wrote 45 years ago.

My love affair with plants has not diminished all these years later. When I moved to Salt Spring Island on the BC coast in 1976, I started to grow foods and herbs a lot more than picking them in the wild. My gardens got larger and larger, and by 1986 I was managing my own seed company, Salt Spring Seeds. I now maintain over 700 plant varieties and ship seeds all over the world. You can find seeds for many of the plants in *Some Useful Wild Plants* in my catalogue at saltspringseeds. com, including alfalfa, burdock, clover, goldenrod, miner's lettuce, nettles, nodding onion, plantain, purslane, St. John's wort, valerian and yarrow!

Whether in the wild or in your own garden, the plants in this book have so much to offer in terms of nutrition, medicine, self-empowerment and beauty. Happy foraging and happy growing!

Dan Jason

Herbs & Shrubs

Alfalfa
Medicago sativa Fabaceae

Alfalfa is sometimes called lucerne or buffalo herb. It is grown in many places for animal feed and is also often seen growing wild in fields. This clover-like plant has a deep taproot, numerous stems, and leaves that appear in threes but are narrower and smaller than clover leaves. It has racemes of small flowers that are usually purple but sometimes yellow.

Alfalfa flowers have been used as a cough remedy, and alfalfa leaves are most commonly used in combination with mint leaves as a food or tonic. The leaves of young plants (best collected in the spring or early summer) can be dried, ground and eaten raw in salad, steeped in hot water as tea or mixed in with prepared cereal. We suggest that the leaves be used as nutrient and tonic: they are an excellent source of vitamins A, B, D, E and K; alfalfa leaves also contain potassium, phosphorous, iron, sodium, silicon, magnesium and many trace elements. Alfalfa is very high in protein (18.9 percent) and calcium, and alfalfa leaves as tea contain no oxalic acid or caffeine. Much more of the protein content can be assimilated if the leaves are put through a grinder first.

Alfalfa

Alum root
Heuchera spp.   Saxifragaceae

Alum root is commonly found in poor soils of exposed mountainsides. At the base of the stem is a group of long-stemmed leaves, which are oval with irregular lobes. A cluster of small yellow flowers blooms in early June along the upper part of the slender, hairy stem. The taproot is surprisingly large.

Young leaves of alum root may be boiled or steamed. Alum root is a strong astringent, and the roots eaten raw are a good remedy for diarrhea. Ground and used as a poultice, the roots' astringency is good for closing wounds. Wet and pounded, the root may be used on sores and swelling. A tonic of the boiled roots is useful for debility and fever. The root is best dug before the plant flowers.

Arrowhead or wapato
Sagittaria latifolia   Alismataceae

Wapato is a bog or water plant of sea-level to subalpine elevations. It is found in ponds, the shallow water of lakes, and slow-moving streams throughout BC. If the water is deep enough, the arrow-shaped leaves don't develop and only long, slender leaf stalks are evident. Flowers, sometimes several feet above the leaves, are in whorls of three; they have three sepals and three waxy white petals. The long stem contains a milky sap. Seed heads are globular. The tubers are quite large and break off easily. The plant may be in the water or erect above it. It flowers in late June or early July.

Wapato tubers can be roasted, boiled or ground into flour. The milky juice of the stem is unpleasant raw but sweet when cooked.

Alum root

Arrowleaf balsamroot or spring sunflower
Balsamorhiza sagittata   Asteraceae

Balsamroot is found throughout the dry Interior on fairly open and dry hills and in valleys with deep, sandy soils. It first appears in early April and begins flowering late in the month. It is often near open ponderosa pine forest with buttercup, mullein, yarrow and biscuitroot. Leaves are large, basal, olive green, smooth-edged and arrow-shaped; they have fine silver-grey hairs and grow on large stalks. Bright yellow ray flowers surround the disc-shaped flowers. Balsamroot's naked stems and silvery appearance distinguish it from sunflower (*Helianthus* spp.). A dozen or so flowers may arise from each bundle of leaves. Roots are often several inches thick, resinous and woody. At flowering, balsamroot is often two feet high.

The entire plant may be used year-round. Young stems and leaves may be boiled and eaten as greens; they become tougher and more fibrous with age. The root may be eaten raw or cooked. We like it sliced and gently stir-fried. Seeds, when roasted, ground and made into mush, have a toasted popcorn flavour.

The root, when peeled, ground and boiled, can be drunk as a remedy for rheumatism and headache. The mashed root can be used for swelling and insect bites. A decoction of the root causes profuse perspiration.

Balsamroot

Biscuitroot

Lomatium spp.

Apiaceae

Biscuitroot is mainly an Interior plant, found on dry plains and hills and frequently at the base of rock cliffs and outcrops. Height is several inches to several feet, depending on the species. Leaves are greatly divided. Flowers are small and in compound umbels coloured white, yellow, pink or purple. There can be one or several stems; the flower stem, often purplish, is leafless. Leaves of most *Lomatium* species smell and taste much like parsley. In several species, the root consists of several large connected bulbs; others have thick, fleshy roots. First flowering is around the beginning of April.

All of the many species have edible roots. A tea can be made from the leaves, stems or flowers. The seeds can be eaten raw, roasted or dried. The roots are better if dug after flowering; they are delicious raw, cooked, dried or ground into flour. The green stems and leaves are good spring salad materials.

Biscuitroot

Bitterroot
Lewisia rediviva   Portulacaceae

Bitterroot grows in dry, rocky open places, flowering at the end of April or in early May in the dry Interior. It has thick, oblong leaves and is nearly stemless. The flowers are rose-pink (sometimes white) and have 10 to 15 petals. It is a perennial with a thick and fleshy carrot-shaped root. The plant often appears leafless because the tufts of leaves may have dried by the time flowers appear.

The root and inner bark are starchy and nutritious. The outer covering can be soaked loose and removed. Cooking takes away most of the bitterness; boil it to a jelly-like consistency.

The pounded dry root was chewed by First Nations foragers to help sore throat.

Bitterroot

Broadleaf cattail
Typha latifolia   Typhaceae

The cattail is very common in moist or wet places such as marshes, shallow ponds, ditches and stream borders. The spongy, dark brown spikes are four to eight inches long and contain the pollen grains. The leaves are long, flat and about an inch wide.

The young shoots pulled from the rootstalks in spring are succulent raw or cooked. They can be gathered throughout summer and fall when still under a foot long. The young flower stalks can be taken out of their sheaths and cooked.

The rootstalks should be obtained after the cattails have turned brown in the fall. After the outer peel has been removed, the core can be eaten raw or cooked. Cattail rootstalks have a very high starch content and can be used to obtain an excellent flour. The difficulty with obtaining the flour as well as with eating the rootstalk is the harsh fibres it contains. These can be removed by drying and pounding the rootstalk cores and then sifting out the fibres. The flour will settle to the bottom if water is used. The flour is about 80 percent carbohydrate and 7 percent protein.

Cattail pollen can be used as stuffing for pillows and blankets, for caulking walls and barrels, and as insulation. The shoots can be used to make mats, baskets and other woven materials. The down makes excellent tinder.

Cattails

Bulrush
Scirpus spp.   Cyperaceae

Bulrushes grow in dense patches in mud or shallow water. They grow from perennial rootstalks and have grass-like leaves or no leaves at all, except for a few sheaths around the stem base. Stems are round to triangular and usually three to nine feet tall. The flowers grow in clusters of spikelets at the head of the stem and have leaf-like bracts.

The starchy rootstalks can be eaten boiled, baked or raw. They should be peeled first. The centre root core is particularly tasty. Rootstalks can also be peeled, dried and pounded into flour. Young shoots, white stem bases and new shoot bulbs are also edible raw or cooked. Bulrush pollen can be gathered and pressed into cakes or used in other ways in baking.

Stalks are generally too tough for eating, but they are useful material for cordage, sandals, baskets and mats.

Bur reed
Sparganium spp.   Sparganiaceae

Bur reeds are found in shallow water or mud, but they seldom form extensive patches. The young plant resembles a large, erect grass with white blossoms. When young, they can be confused with cattails; however, but bur reed flowers are not in terminal spikes but in round heads, mainly at the side of the stems. Height can be up to seven feet. Like the bulrush, bur reed flowers during July and August. Flowers are replaced by round seed heads resembling burrs.

Bulbous stem bases and tuberous roots can be used for food in much the same way as those of the bulrush.

Burdock
Arctium spp.   Asteraceae

Burdock is common in moist, exposed areas and near and around buildings. It has a thick stem with many branches. The leaves are very large and woolly underneath. Flowers are bristly and purplish. By fall, the top of the plant is covered with hard, round and very sticky burrs.

The young leaves and shoots can be cooked as greens or eaten raw, but they are not very palatable. The young stems and flower stalk can be peeled down to the pith and included with the leaves. The root, too, is edible if one wants to go to the trouble of peeling away the tough rind. It can also be roasted and ground as a delicious coffee substitute.

Medicinally, burdock is used as a tonic and a blood purifier. Some authors recommend it for skin conditions like eczema and syphilis, and externally as a salve or a wash for skin irritations or burns. A leaf infusion tones the stomach, serves as a mild laxative and may help long-term indigestion. For severe pain, one author recommends bruising and rolling up the green leaves, dipping them in hot vinegar and covering the skin with them and a hot woollen cloth.

Burdock's chemical constituents include inulin, tannic acid, vitamin C, iron and niacin.

Illustration next page

INWOOD ♀ '71

Burdock

Camas
Camassia spp.   Liliaceae

Although camas supposedly only grows west of the Cascades, we have found much of it in the southern Columbia River Valley, particularly near Castlegar. On southern Vancouver Island and the Gulf Islands, it prefers moist, rich ground—generally near arbutus and Garry oak. Leaves of camas are basal, grass-like and eight to 15 inches long. Flowers appear in early May and are usually a brilliant blue (though there are occasionally white ones); they are on a single stalk and have three sepals and three petals. The plant grows to two feet on the coast and three feet in the Interior. The root bulb is ovate. Flower colour is crucial for identification; the poisonous death camas, which is frequently found with camas, has yellow or greenish-white flowers and a similar stalk and leaves.

First Nations people marked flowering plants with bark strips and returned in August to dig up the bulbs. They cooked bulbs in pits of hot ashes for an entire day, stripped the bark and pressed the bulbs flat like pancakes. The bulbs smell like vanilla and taste like brown sugar or maple sugar. Molasses can be made from the bulbs by boiling them until the water has almost completely evaporated.

Camas bulb is purgative and emetic if eaten to excess.

Camomile
Chamaemelum nobile   Asteraceae

Camomile (or chamomile) looks like yellow-headed daisies. One species has petals, another doesn't. It grows low in hard-packed open ground around houses, in old dirt roadways, and along highways.

The flower heads and leaves are delicious as tea and as herb beer.

An infusion of camomile is consumed as a remedy for nightmares, insomnia and nervousness in general. It is a popular remedy for indigestion, heartburn and loss of appetite (especially in combination with ginger root, drunk cold). It is also good for colic and preventing children's summer diarrhea.

Externally, camomile can be used as a poultice for swelling and inflammatory pain, especially in the throat or neck. It is good as a lotion for toothache and earache and as a wash for sore, weak eyes and open sores or wounds.

We enjoy camomile in a bath or as an herbal shampoo, either by itself or mixed with other herbs. Rubbed on the skin in a boiled-down decoction or tincture, it is said to work as an insect repellant and to ease pain and swelling from insect bites.

The decocted herb is supposed to yield a blond dye.

Camomile

Chickweed
Stellaria media and *Cerastium* spp.   Caryophyllaceae

Chickweed grows throughout BC in shaded areas, waste ground, fields, salty or sandy soil, etc. It flowers in early spring in small, white leafy clusters; flowers have five petals, each of which is cleft in two. The stem of many species is weak, reclining and tufted with hairs. *Stellaria media* has a line of hairs running up one side of the stem; the upper leaves are sessile and the lower ones are stalked. Chickweed often forms a leafy, mat-like growth from three inches to a foot high.

Chickweed can be eaten raw or cooked. It is rich in iron, especially the upper leaf portion. The young tips can be cooked like spinach.

Chickweed is a good healer and soother for all types of external and internal irritations. The bruised leaves in coconut or other oil make a good ointment for skin irritation. Chickweed is considered a remedy for an irritated digestive system, ulcers, internal inflammation, irritated genitals, skin sores and eye sties. It can be used as a tea, a lotion or a poultice held in place by larger leaves such as mullein. It is also useful for coughs, hoarseness and minor lung irritation. Chickweed baths are soothing.

Chickweed

Chicory
Cichorium intybus   Asteraceae

Chicory (or succory, or bachelor's buttons) is a common roadside plant. It can be easily identified when it flowers in midsummer in blue dandelion-like heads. It prefers dry open ground, has long wiry stems, and has leaves at the base similar to dandelion leaves.

The young leaves and shoots are commonly used in salads and as a pot-herb (especially blanched to remove the slight bitterness), and the roots are eaten raw or roasted. Chicory is often used with coffee or as a coffee substitute, along with dandelion and burdock roots. (Gather older roots of these plants, slice, roast and grind.)

Chicory is especially rich in vitamins A and C.

A tea made from the root is said to be good for an upset stomach and kidney and liver complaints. The bruised leaves can be used as a poultice for swelling and inflammation. A syrup made from the root is reportedly a good laxative for children.

Chicory

Cinquefoil
Potentilla spp.   Rosaceae

There are over 20 species of cinquefoil (meaning "five finger") in BC. The characteristic features of the various cinquefoils are the yellow buttercup-like flowers and the five-fingered toothed leaves on branched stalks. Some species are several feet tall, while others are small and shrubby.

Cinquefoil roots can be eaten like potatoes—boiled or roasted. Tea made from the roots is a little bitter.

Medicinally, the root is used in lotions, gargles and syrups, and as an infusion. The root is boiled in vinegar to be used for sores and inflammation, decocted with honey for hoarseness and coughs, and boiled in wine to ease pain in the joints. It is known to reduce bleeding and is used both externally and internally for this purpose. It is also used as an eyewash, for diarrhea, for cramps in the stomach or lungs (taken both internally and as a compress), for colic, for ulcers in the stomach, for toothache and for spongy gums and loose teeth.

Cinquefoil

Clover
Trifolium spp.   Fabaceae

Clover is a familiar wayside plant with leaflets of three and flower heads of purple, pink, white or yellow.

The whole plant is edible, although the raw flowers are hard to digest in quantity. (More flowers can be eaten if cooked or soaked for several hours in strong salt water.) Its high protein content makes clover very nutritious. The seeds and flowers are excellent steeped in boiled water as tea. (Leaves and flowers should never be boiled, as boiling destroys vitamins; instead, pour boiling water over the leaves or flowers. Roots and other hard plant parts usually need to be boiled.)

Clover tea is good for colds, coughs, bronchitis and nervous conditions. One cough syrup uses flowers, onion juice and warm honey; another uses flowers, new sprigs of white pine, mullein leaves, cherry bark and honey. Flowers, boiled and applied as a poultice, are said to be a remedy for athlete's foot.

Red clover

Clustered broomrape
Orobanche fasiculata   Orobanchaceae

Broomrape grows in dry, sandy soil mainly east of the Cascades. It is parasitic on the roots of other plants such as sagebrush. It is usually purple-tinged but may be yellowish. Leaves are scale-like and in an alternate pattern. Flowers, first appearing in early May, are two-lipped, sticky and hairy. The stem is very scaly and coarse-haired. Broomrape can grow several feet high.

The entire plant, including the roots, can be eaten raw or roasted. The juice or a decoction of young branches or seeds, or just the powdered seed, is supposed to ease pain of the joints and hips and swelling of the spleen, as well as cleanse the kidneys and bladder. The plant has been used as a tooth-ache remedy, to kill lice, and as a skin cleanser (decocted or boiled in oil).

Coltsfoot or butterbur
Petasites spp.   Asteraceae

Coltsfoot leaves may be triangular, kidney-shaped or almost round depending on the species. They are entirely basal, toothed and often deeply cleft, white, woolly underneath and often a foot across. Flowers are purplish-white, sweet-scented and in soft loose heads on the ends of long, scaly-bracted stalks. They appear in March or soon after the snow is gone, sometimes before the leaves grow. Coltsfoot has a thick, creeping rootstalk and grows to a height of two feet.

The young foliage and flowers make a good pot-herb. Salt can be obtained by wilting the leaves in hot sun, rolling them with the stems into tight balls and ashing them on cedar bark over slow coals. The ashes are almost pure salt.

Another plant termed coltsfoot is *Tussilago farfara*. It also blooms in early spring before leaves appear and has large, toothed, basal leaves that are white and woolly underneath; the flower stalk consists of numerous scale-like leaves. The leaves are round, and the flowers have numerous ray flowers. It prefers moist, heavy soils and is reported only on Vancouver Island. This coltsfoot has been much used in cough and lung medicines and smoking mixtures.

Coltsfoot

Comfrey
Symphytum officinale

Boraginaceae

Comfrey (also called knitbone) is a perennial that's seldom found wild in BC, but because of its potential importance and easy cultivation, we have included it. The root is oblong and fleshy, the tall stalk hollow and covered with prickly hairs. The lower leaves are large and covered with rough hair, which causes itching; the leaves decrease in size as they grow up the stem. Pairs of drooping flowers, which are creamy yellow or purple, bloom most of the summer. Comfrey grows best in low, moist ground.

The whole plant is used externally as a hot poultice to reduce swollen parts around fractured bones and to soothe pain in any other tender, inflamed part. (This includes insect bites, sprains, bruises, sore breasts, boils and ulcers.) Internally, the root can be used in a decoction for ulcers, lung troubles, coughing and nasal congestion, and as a gentle remedy for diarrhea. The known healing agent it contains is allantoin—a cell proliferant contained in both the leaves and the root.

Comfrey is also used for tanning leather and as a glue.

Comfrey

Dandelion
Taraxacum officinale   Asteraceae

Some of the uses of dandelion are well known. The young leaves can be used in salads, boiled as nettles or cooked in soup (especially blanched). The dried leaves can be used to make herb beer or tea. The flowers can be used to decorate or flavour various cooked dishes or to make wine. The roots can be cooked as a vegetable. The crown of blanched leaf stems on top of the root is delicious. Old roots can be dried, roasted and ground for a coffee.

Dandelion greens are a blood tonic and a stimulant for the whole body. They have been found to have a pronounced stimulating effect on the digestive system, liver, kidneys and bowels.

Dandelion root is slightly laxative and has been used as a remedy for jaundice, skin diseases and eczema. The juice of the stem and flower is supposed to be a remedy for warts (touch the juice to the wart and allow it to dry).

Dandelion greens contain large amounts of vitamin A (7,000 international units/ounce); vitamins B, C and E; sodium, potassium and magnesium salts.

Dandelion root contains more of its active properties (taraxacin and inulin) in the autumn and should be gathered then. The root should be dried whole for about two weeks until hard and brittle, and (like any dried herb) kept in a dry place. Dandelion greens are best gathered before the flower stalks start.

Dandelion

Devil's club
Oplopanax horridus   Araliaceae

This prickly shrub is an all-too-familiar sight in the back-woods near streams and rivers. The stalks are tall and thick with sharp spines that produce lingering pain on contact, and the leaves are maple-shaped and prickly. Greenish flowers develop into scarlet fruit.

The young stems can be eaten as a pot-herb, and the root can be peeled and chewed raw.

Medicinally, the plant is good for colds and rheumatism when the bark and thorns are peeled away and the stalk is used for tea. Baby talc can be made by drying and pulverizing the bark. The root bark of devil's club has been found to reduce blood sugar and thus be effective in the treatment of diabetes.

The root is also reportedly excellent for treating staph infections (used both externally and internally). It is a strong laxative.

Elderberry
Sambucus spp.   Caprifoliaceae

Many people know the elder shrub from using its berries for elderberry wine. When in bloom in the summer, it is easily identified by its flat white head of flowers, which is about five to eight inches across. The leaflets are sharp-pointed, willow-like, opposite and usually in nines in the blueberry elder and fives and sevens in the blackberry elder. The blackberry elder is usually found above 4,000 feet; the blueberry elder is most common in the BC Interior. Redberry elderberries are not palatable.

Elderberries can be steeped raw in cold water for a refreshing drink, in hot wine with honey, or canned and drunk in the winter. They are one of the richest natural sources of vitamin C. The flower, too, can make a delicious beverage, usually a tea.

Elder leaves and flowers can be made into an ointment for bruises, sprains and wounds. Bruised or decocted, they are said to drive away flies and other insects. They also help in the treatment of poison ivy rash. The flowers can also be used for coughs, colds and sore throat (combined with honey and vinegar), as a laxative and as a general remedy and tonic.

Elder bark can be used to quickly cleanse the system through the bowels and bladder, and by vomiting. It contains sambunigrin—a cyanogenic glycoside—which is poisonous if absorbed. Hot elderberry wine with honey is a popular remedy for colds, and the berries steeped as tea are reportedly good for diarrhea.

Occultists claim elder is surrounded by a wide healing aura; it used to be common practice to plant an elder near the house as protection against disease and evil spirits, or to carry an elder twig for good luck and health.

Illustration next page

Elderberry

False Solomon's seal
Smilacina racemosa

Asparagaceae

False Solomon's seal (or wild spinach, as it is known in the Slocan Valley) is found in damp, shady places throughout BC. A plume of fragrant, creamy flowers blooming in May and June tops the stem of two rows of alternate broad glossy leaves from 2.5 to 6 inches long. Greenish-red berries are ripe in late July and August.

Some say the berries are tasteless, but they seem to us to taste like the fresh leaves. Both the leaves and young shoots are delicious raw or as a pot-herb.

The thick fleshy rootstalk can be grated and made into a poultice for wounds. It is also said to be a laxative and a remedy for rheumatism. The seeds eaten in quantity cleanse the bowels.

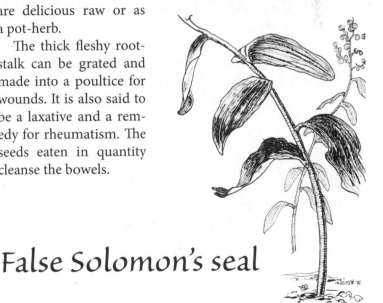

False Solomon's seal

Ferns

Dennstaedtiaceae

Bracken fern (*Pteridium aquilinum pubescens*) is the most wide-ranging fern in BC. Stems, unlike those of most ferns, do not cluster from a compact base. Leaf margins have lines of spore cases. Bracken fern is found in moist coniferous forests at low elevations from Vancouver Island to the Rockies. During early spring, the young shoots of bracken fern uncurl in juicy stalks called fiddleheads. These can be eaten raw, cooked like asparagus or used in soups. Roasted roots can also be eaten if the outer skin is stripped and the insides pounded to separate the fibre from the edible part. They contain much starch and are best dug in autumn. It is wise to avoid eating large amounts of raw fiddleheads because they contain an enzyme, thiaminase, that destroys thiamine in the body. This can result in vitamin B1 deficiency. (Cooking deactivates thiaminase.)

The rhizomes of swordfern (*Polystichum munitum*) can be roasted and used as food, as can those of bracken fern. Swordfern forms dark green symmetrical fronds up to three feet long. The pinnules, or side leaves, are sharp-pointed and sharp-toothed, and the underside is brownish from the twin rows of spore cases. Swordfern is found on Vancouver Island and the Gulf Islands, and in coastal forests.

Several other ferns have rootstalks that can be roasted for food. These include lady fern (*Athyrium filix-femina*) and deer fern (*Struthiopteris spicant*). Polypody or licorice fern (*Polypodium* spp.)—a small fern found on mossy cliffs, logs and tree trunks—has thickish roots that have a licorice flavour when chewed raw. This has been used as a uterine tonic. Dried roots, boiled to a syrup in water, have been used as a cough medicine.

Bracken fern

Fireweed
Epilobium angustifolium   Onagraceae

Fireweed prefers fairly rich, moist soil on old burns, in cleared-out areas, along streams and in open woods and thickets. It is usually two to six feet high and has long willow-like, lance-shaped leaves, which alternate on the stem. The flowers, in long terminal clusters, are a beautiful pink-purple and bloom through most of the summer. It develops seed pods that split open to release hundreds of fluffy white seeds.

The young shoots and flower buds can be eaten raw or boiled. The pith of the stalks can be nibbled and, dried and boiled, is good in soups. The leaves, green or dry, make a good tonic tea, especially combined with other herbs.

Fireweed has been used internally for piles and diarrhea, eczema, sore throat, colon troubles and diseases of the mucous membranes. Externally, it has been used for painful joints and rheumatism. The root, grated and made into a poultice, is supposed to be an excellent remedy for ulcerated sores.

To separate the filaments from the mealy portions, the root should be thoroughly dried, cut up and pounded.

Fireweed

Garlic
Allium sativum

Amaryllidaceae

Garlic, like parsley, is worth cultivating indoors and having fresh year-round. Although it grows wild, it is not very common and is difficult to distinguish from other *Allium* species in BC.

As food, garlic is high in vitamins A, B and C and in sulphur, iron and calcium.

As medicine, garlic is useful for all bodily disorders. It stimulates healthful bacteria and suppresses unhealthful ones. It rids the body of worms, lowers blood pressure and slows aging. Crushed and boiled in milk, it allays nervous spasms and seizures. Garlic is useful for treating rheumatism and arthritis, and for general disease protection. It is also used for flatulence, intestinal disorders, skin wounds and diseases, insect stings and skin ailments caused by parasites. It is reportedly excellent as a poultice for staph infections and ringworm. It is helpful when applied to canker sores and aching teeth.

Garlic is a good fungicide; it kills mosquito larvae and is toxic to a number of insects.

Ginger
Asarum caudatum   Aristolochiaceae

Look for wild ginger in damp places and beside creeks and rivers. The plant has a distinct ginger smell, especially the root, which is the part most often used. Ginger sends out runners much like strawberries do. Fine hairs cover the stem and veins and the lower margin of the heart-shaped leaves. It has a bell-like purplish-brown flower, which stays very close to the ground and appears in spring.

The rootstalk of wild ginger can be used instead of commercial ginger. It can be made into a refreshing tea (about half an ounce of root to one pint of boiling water) or candied. (Boil in water until tender, then boil short pieces in a heavy syrup.)

The root is used for chronic chest complaints, bowel and stomach spasms, diarrhea, head colds, sore throat and suppressed menstruation. It serves to tone and stimulate the whole body. The root is aromatic and could be used as a scent in linens or a bath or hair rinse.

Ginger is best collected in the fall. Chemical constituents include two strong antibiotics.

Wild ginger

Glasswort or pickleweed
Salicornia herbacea, ambigua and *europaea*   Amaranthaceae

Glasswort is found in saline and alkaline soil, on coastal beaches and tidal flats, and near bogs, marshes and lakes. From a distance, it looks like a grass. It has opposite, fleshy, scale-like leaves. Flowers are small and grow at the joints in cylindrical spikes of three to seven; they have one or two stamens. The opposite-branching stem is fleshy and jointed.

The shoots and tops of glasswort are succulent and make a good salad. They are very salty. Glasswort can be used pickled or as a seasoning, and it is edible spring, summer and fall. Because of its high sodium content, it has been used in both soap-making and glass-making.

Glasswort

Goldenrod
Solidago spp.   Asteraceae

Goldenrod grows in rich soil along roads, trails and streams, and in open forest. The flowers form small yellow pyramids at the top of the stem, which is a foot or taller. Like those of fireweed, the leaves alternate, and they are long and willow-like.

The young leaves can be used in salads or as a pot-herb, the seeds for mush and thickening soups, and the dried leaves and flowers for a delicious, full-bodied tea (one teaspoon dried herb to one cup of boiled water).

Goldenrod is an astringent useful for cleaning sores.

A good yellow dye can be made from the blossoms, and the sap is high in rubber content. In other parts of the world the plant has been cultivated as a natural rubber.

Goldenrod

Ground ivy
Glechoma hederacea Lamiaceae

Ground ivy is a creeping perennial herb that often forms a ground cover in shaded, moist forests in southern BC. The hairy stems are square and jointed, bearing leaves in pairs and roots at each joint or node. The opposite leaves are round to kidney-shaped, hairy and stalked, and have toothed margins. Flowers are blue to purplish, half to one inch long and usually paired in the axils of the upper leaves. The flowering portion of the stem is often erect, but generally the plant doesn't rise more than half a foot above the ground. Flowers appear in May, and the plant continues to blossom for several months. The whole plant possesses a strong mint aroma and has a bitter taste.

Like many members of the mint family, ground ivy is recommended as a digestive tonic and a cough remedy. It is a good source of vitamin C. It is best ingested as a tea infusion of the freshly picked plant. Cold and unsweetened, the tea can also be used as a bitter tonic to stimulate the appetite.

Gumweed
Grindelia spp.   Asteraceae

Gumweed is a low plant of open spaces found in dry, somewhat saline soil. In late July and August, it has bright yellow flowers on rough, sticky burrs. The burrs each have five to six rows of very gummy bracts. Leaves are alternate, stiff and oblong. Lower leaves are gone by flowering time. Coastal species (*G. stricta, G. nana* and *G. integrifolia*) are robust and much branched; those found in saline meadows of the Interior (*G. nana* and *G. squarrosa*) are spindly and less branched.

Gumweed leaves can be used as tea or chewed. First Nations foragers boiled the roots for liver complaints and used the upper third of the plant as a stomach tonic and anti-spasmodic. It was also much used to relieve ivy and oak poisoning. Today, a fluid extract from the flowering tops and leaves is officially used by Western medicine to treat the above ailments. Gumweed has an anti-spasmodic effect similar to atropine. A broth of leaves (especially the sticky part) is good for indigestion, sore throat, coughs, colds and congestion. Externally, a leaf decoction is excellent for running sores, itching, wounds, ulcers, rheumatism and toothache.

Horsetail

Equisetum spp.   Equisetaceae

Horsetails (foxtails, scouring rush and joint grass) are found in moist soil along streams and rivers, and in marshes and other damp places. Horsetail has a ridged green stem divided into sections by dark, narrow bands. The hollow stems pull apart easily. Horsetails are of two kinds—one sterile and many-branched, the other fertile and unbranched. The top of the fertile plant has a brown head.

The young shoots of the horsetail can be used in spring as a pot-herb but later become too stiff and unpalatable. The tough outer tissue of the stem can be peeled away and the sweet pulp eaten raw. Horsetail plants have been known to poison livestock so should be eaten sparingly. Another reason to consume only small amounts of them is that horsetail plants contain thiaminase, which reduces thiamine in the body (see information under Ferns).

A decoction of horsetail is good for stopping and healing bleeding wounds if applied as a poultice. Horsetail is also used to reduce swelling of the eyelids, to heal ulcers inside the urinary and digestive tracts, as a stimulant in kidney disorders and for menstrual disorders.

The older silicon-covered rushes can be used in sharpening, polishing and honing, and as sandpaper.

Horsetail

Kinnikinnick
Arctostaphylos uva-ursi   Ericaceae

Kinnikinnick is also known as arbutus uva-ursi, manzanita, and bearberry. It is a very common shrub that forms a low green mat in the woods, along roads, and in dry, exposed places. The plant is usually two to four feet high. The evergreen leaves are thick and leathery, grow alternately along the stem and are half an inch to one inch long. Bell-shaped pink flowers bloom in spring, and bright red berries dot the glossy leaves from August to winter.

Kinnikinnick berries are high in vitamin C and have a bittersweet flavour. They become much sweeter when cooked and are reportedly good in sauces and jams. The raw leaves can be chewed to prevent thirst or used as a tea to tone the body.

Medicinally, an infusion of kinnikinnick leaves is most helpful for its antiseptic effect on the urinary passages, bladder and kidneys. It is especially good in combination with dandelion greens.

Kinnikinnick is very popular as a tobacco substitute, usually mixed with other herbs such as mullein, sage, snowbrush or ordinary tobacco.

Illustration page 147

Labrador tea
Rhododendron groenlandicum   Ericaceae

Labrador tea is an evergreen shrub that grows in cold bogs and on wet, rocky hillsides. It is a common ground cover in northwestern BC and is also common on the west coast of Vancouver Island. It has irregular, woolly branches and grows to about four feet. Leaves are narrow and thick, with a smooth upper side and a woolly mat of brownish-red hairs on the underside; these are usually one to two inches long and have rolled edges. Leaves are grouped, giving them a rough whorl-like look. In southern BC, the flowers bloom in June; they have five white petals and appear in terminal clusters one to two inches wide. Flowers are replaced by clusters of dry husks that often hang on through winter.

Labrador tea leaves are best picked before flowering, then dried, crushed and steeped for tea. They have a pleasant odour, a spicy taste and slight narcotic properties. The leaves can be smoked for a similar effect; large amounts can cause headache. Labrador tea is said to be good for sore throat or chest congestion and for cough. Several authors, however, warn of poisonous properties because of the compound andromedotoxin (also found in rhododendrons and laurels). The plant has in fact been used as a moth and mouse repellant, and in strong decoction as a wash to kill lice. It is also reportedly good in a lotion to relieve the sting and itch of mosquito bites.

Mountain Labrador tea (*Ledum glandulosum*) is a somewhat similar shrub with larger deciduous leaves whose undersides are pale and resin-dotted. It is found on shady, damp mountain slopes mostly east of the Cascades and has properties similar to those of Labrador tea.

Lamb's quarters
Chenopodium spp.   Amaranthaceae

Lamb's quarters is a garden weed as tasty and nutritious as anything cultivated in the garden. It is just as popularly known as pigweed and is found in almost any dry field at low elevation where the soil has been turned up. The leaves are diamond-shaped and dark green, and radiate out from the stem in four directions when low and in branches and more directions when taller. If allowed to grow, it may reach two or more feet in height.

The younger the leaves and shoots are, the better. Lamb's quarters can be used as salad or cooked like nettles. The plant is very high in vitamins A and C but contains oxalic acid and oil of chenopodium, so should not be eaten in large quantities. The seeds are edible if ground for meal.

We have found that, bruised and applied to the forehead, lamb's quarters leaves are excellent for removing heat from too much sun, headache, etc. They can be used in the same way for eye inflammation. The plant is also reportedly useful for stomach ailments.

Lamb's quarters

Mallow
Malva neglecta and other species   Malvaceae

Mallow is found in waste places and cultivated fields throughout BC. Leaves are alternate and nearly round (kidney-shaped in *Malva neglecta*). Flowers have five sepals and five petals, which appear singly or clustered; these are pink, bluish or whitish depending on the species. Flowering occurs in May or June. Each flower gives rise to a group of 12 to 15 distinct outlets (carpels) that form a disc looking somewhat like a peeled orange.

Young leaves are good in salad. Older leaves and stems, if boiled, may take some getting used to. The seed pods ("cheeses") are good. "Marshmallow" is taken from the dried powdered root and used in confectionery. No species of mallow is poisonous.

A poultice made from the leaves, stems and flowers is useful for sores, inflammation, swelling, bruises, skin eruptions, etc. An infusion of mallow is good for bowel, kidney and urinary tract inflammation, as well as for coughs, colds and teething. With honey, it can relieve eye inflammation.

Mallow

Milkweed
Asclepias spp. especially *speciosa*   Apocynaceae

Milkweed is found on open ground in the driest parts of the province. It grows to a height of two to four feet on a finely hairy unbranched stem. Leaves are thick, fleshy, opposite and oblong, and grow to six inches in length; they are finely hairy underneath. Flowering is in late June or early July. Flowers are purplish and bunched together in knobby heads; they have five petals and five curved horns. Long seed pods contain flat seeds with long, silky hairs. Pods open in the fall to release thousands of silky parachutes. A nick in the stem or leaves produces a characteristic milky fluid. Look for milkweed along the highway near Ashcroft, Merritt, Kamloops, Oliver, Osoyoos and Keremeos.

Milkweed flowers are edible raw or cooked. The pods, when light green and soft, and the flowers in full bloom are good prepared as fritters or included in soup or stew. Five-to-six-inch-high shoots are good when prepared like asparagus. Milkweed is rich in vitamin C. The flowers can be boiled down into a sugar. Moderation is necessary, as a number of the species are poisonous to various degrees, but normal quantities of *A. speciosa* are safe. Seeds contain 20 percent edible oil similar to soybean oil.

Milkweed fluid is effective when applied to warts, corns, calluses, ringworm, wounds and sores. The seeds can also be ground and made into a salve for sores. An infusion of the leaves can be drunk for sore breasts and to increase lactation. The roots in boiling water are supposed to relieve cough, fever and catarrh.

Miner's lettuce
Montia perfoliata and *sibirica*   Montiaceae

Two species of miner's lettuce are common in BC. *Montia perfoliata* has saucer-shaped upper leaves through which the stem protrudes. Its small white flowers grow from stems arising from the centre of the leaf discs. *Montia sibirica* (Siberian miner's lettuce) has short-stemmed upper leaves. Its flowers, on long thin stems, have five notched petals bearing thin red lines. Lower leaves of both species have long stems. Both species are common on Vancouver Island and the coastal mainland. *M. perfoliata* is common in the Okanagan; *M. sibirica* is found in the Kootenay and Arrow Lakes regions. (*Montia* species are somewhat similar to species of *Claytonia,* such as spring beauty, but the *Montia* genus doesn't have corms.)

Stems, leaves and roots of miner's lettuce are delicious raw or cooked. The plant is in bloom and suitable for eating in April and May.

Illustrations next page

Siberian miner's lettuce

Miner's lettuce

Mint

Spearmint (*Mentha spicata*)   Lamiaceae
Horehound (*Marrubium vulgare*)
Peppermint (*Mentha piperita*)
Canada mint (*Mentha arvensis*)

These mint family plants all have a square stem and opposite leaves. The flowers are just above each set of leaves and range from white through pink and purple. Menthol is derived from *M. arvensis,* spearmint from *M. spicata,* and peppermint from *M. piperita.* Probably the best way to tell them apart is by smell or taste. Horehound prefers much drier ground than the other mints. Spearmint tends to have darker leaves that are less deeply toothed than Canada mint and grows taller. Both these and peppermint grow in moist ground and are often found in bog-like areas near rivers.

All of the mints make very refreshing teas, flavouring agents, and scents. They are soothing for colds, sore throat, hiccuping, toothache and coughs (especially with elderflowers and yarrow). Mints are also good for nausea, seasickness, colic, flatulence, indigestion, headache, heartburn, convulsions and spasms in infants, and other nervous upsets. Horehound is often made into candy or syrup to use for children's coughs, colds and colic. It has been used for expelling worms. Rats and mice strongly dislike peppermint, so it can be used to repel them. A remedy for children's teething pain consists of peppermint and skullcap infused together, strained and drunk cold.

Illustration next page

SPEARMINT

PEPPERMINT

INWOOD '71

Mints

Monkey flower
Mimulus guttatus

Phrymaceae

Yellow monkey flowers are found near streams and in moist ground on Vancouver Island, in the Coast Mountains region, in central BC and in the Rockies.

The plant grows almost to the timberline. Leaves are opposite and ovate or rounded; lower leaves have stalks, but not upper ones. The snapdragon-like flowers are yellow and two-lipped, and have purple or brown dots at the throat. The stem is erect, hollow and reddish. The plant is a perennial, usually attaining a height of two feet.

Young leaves and stems can be eaten raw or cooked but are usually bitter when raw.

Raw stems and leaves can be applied as a poultice to burns and wounds. Monkey flower is also useful for treating dysentery and diarrhea.

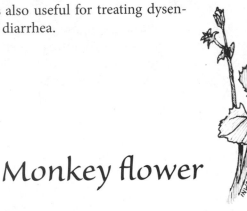

Monkey flower

Mullein
Verbascum thapsus   Scrophulariaceae

Mullein, sometimes called velvet plant or mullein dock, is easily spotted along highways. It has large, light-green, velvety leaves that are like hairy blotting paper. They are often a foot wide. The stem can be as much as five feet high and is topped by a long spike of individual yellow flowers, usually blooming a few at a time from July on. Mullein is very common on arid land.

Although mullein is not useful as a food, it has many medicinal uses. The leaves can be smoked to relieve irritation and congestion of the respiratory mucous membranes and to relieve coughing. The oil of the fresh flowers is good for earache, and steeped in a vegetable oil for a few weeks is supposed to remove rough warts if applied as a poultice. A brew of the whole plant can be used for swollen testicles and scrotum, and a decoction of the root can be used for persistent coughs, toothache, cramps and convulsions. Mullein is also recommended for inflammation from piles, ulcers, tumours, mumps, tonsils, sore throat and chapped skin. The leaves burned as incense help relieve lung congestion.

The leaves are useful as lamp wicks, blotting paper and toilet paper, for cooking in firepits (as a container for vegetables) and as gloves for gathering plants such as nettle.

Mullein

Mustards

Brassica juncea, nigra, kaber and related spp.   Brassicaceae

Mustards are common plants of open fields, meadows and waste grounds. They have large, showy, yellow flowers in open, unbranched clusters that have four petals and four sepals. Lower leaves are stalked and deeply lobed; upper leaves have shorter or no stalks and are unlobed but coarsely toothed. Pods spread from the main stem, and seeds are usually red-brown. Pods in several species have a beak a quarter to half an inch long. Mustards are usually several feet tall.

Mustards are high in vitamins A, B1, B2 and C as well as minerals and protein. Young lower leaves—but not those of the flower stalk—are best. Moderation is urged; if eaten raw and in quantity, they can cause vomiting and diarrhea. The seeds are toxic, with irritant oils.

As medicine, mustard seeds are stimulant, irritant and carminative. *B. nigra* reddens the skin and produces blisters; it is used as a flavouring, stimulant and tonic. Mustards in general are used for poor appetite, flatulence, bad breath, catarrh, rheumatic and arthritic pains, and stiffness. They can also be used in stimulating baths and as plasters.

Nettle
Urtica spp.   Urticaceae

Nettle grows at the edge of moist, shady places. Leaves are coarsely toothed and in pairs; green-white flowers droop in clusters from the stalk. Nettle is covered with small, stinging barbs.

Nettle is popular as a food in many places. As a pot-herb, it is best to use the young tops before the plant flowers. (Gather the tops wearing gloves or using mullein leaves; wash them in running water hanging from a stick. Cook them in their own juice in a saucepan with the lid on until just tender.) The roots are reportedly good roasted. Nettle also makes a good herb beer, and the tea is delicious and nutritious.

Nettle is rich with vitamins A, C and D (it's one of the few plants that contain vitamin D—necessary for assimilation of calcium and bone development). It also contains large amounts of iron, sodium, potassium, phosphorous, calcium and silica.

An infusion of fresh nettle leaves is soothing and healing for burns and hives. The fresh juice aids healing when applied on open wounds of all kinds. Nettle is useful for fevers and head colds, migraines, high blood pressure and anemia, and as a blood purifier. The seeds and juice of the leaves are an antidote for insect stings and bites and some poisonous plants. Nettle can also be used as a wash for itchy crotch and as a hair wash and tonic.

Nettle stalks are widely used for making thread and cloth. The roots yield a yellow dye. Juice produced from boiling the plant with salt is a good substitute for rennet.

Nodding onion
Allium cernuum   Amaryllidaceae

The nodding onion is usually about a foot high and has a bent flower head of about a dozen pink-purple flowers that bloom from June through July. It is most often found on exposed mountainsides. The leaves are grass-like, rising from a thin bulb. The plant is odiferous and can often be smelled before it is seen.

Both the bulb and the flowers are edible, cooked or raw. We like them simmered with brown rice and vegetables. Nodding onion contains vitamins A, B and C, phosphorous, calcium, magnesium, sulphur, sodium, potassium, iron, starch, acetic and phosphoric acids, a hormone called glucokinin, and traces of iodine, zinc and silicon. Overeating nodding onions leads to anemia. In very large quantities, they are poisonous.

Nodding onions stimulate digestive secretions of the pancreas, are a good antiseptic cleanser of the system, and are good for colds characterized by watery eyes and runny nose. Nodding onions are also reportedly good for headache, toothache, earache and eye inflammation. Sucking on a piece of nodding onion effectively relieves coughing and sore throat, and a few drops of onion juice dropped in the ear is excellent in the night for relieving a child's earache. Onion juice rubbed between the toes is said to be good for athlete's foot, and the smashed leaves rubbed on the arms and neck are an effective insect repellent.

Onions have been found to emit a particular type of radiation called mitogenetic radiation, which appears to stimulate cell activity in general and produce a rejuvenating effect on the system. Garlic also emits mitogenetic radiation, and penicillin has a similarly charged electrical field.

Orach
Atriplex spp.

Amaranthaceae

Orach, or seaside lamb's quarters, grows to four to five feet in the sandy soil above the high-water mark on the BC coast. Like lamb's quarters, its leaves are triangular, dark green and one to three inches long.

Orach is rich in vitamins and minerals. It is tender and delicious raw or simmered like spinach. Young, tender leaves can be picked throughout summer and fall.

Orach

Oregon grape
Berberis or *Mahonia* spp.   Berberidaceae

Oregon grape is an evergreen shrub with compound holly-like leaves, clusters of yellow flowers, and blue berries. It commonly grows in woods and on hillsides in wetter regions of BC. It is sometimes called mahonia or barberry.

Flower buds, blossoms and berries are all edible raw, in jam, or in tea. The berries are sweeter after the first frost. Sweetened with honey, the juice tastes like grape juice.

The root and bark of Oregon grape are of special use in treating blood impurities, poor digestion, chronic mucus complaints and coughs. A decoction of the bark is said to be good for washing sores on the skin and in the mouth. A cold tea is a good bitter tonic.

Oregon grape roots and bark yield a yellow dye.

Oregon grape

Ox-eye daisy
Chrysanthemum leucanthemum   Asteraceae

Most of the summer, ox-eye daisies can be seen along road-sides and in the fields throughout southern BC. The plants have slender stems, small-toothed leaves, and flowers with white petals and yellow centres.

The young leaves can be used much as dandelion and chicory leaves can: in salads or as a pot-herb. The flowers can be made into a mild tea.

The leaves and flowers of ox-eye daisy can be used in a soothing tonic; in a lotion for wounds, bruises and ulcers; to relieve coughing; and as an insect powder.

INWOOD ♀ '71

Ox-eye daisy

Parsley
Petroselinum crispum or *Apium petroselinum* Apiaceae

Parsley isn't a wild plant, but it can easily be cultivated in pots and used year-round.

As a food, it is very high in vitamins A and C and is higher in iron than any other green. Digestion time is only one-and-a-quarter hours, much less than for most other foods. It is delicious raw, alone or with other greens, and as a seasoning.

Parsley can be made into a good tonic and is useful for bladder and kidney disorders, rheumatism, arthritis and swollen breasts; as a poultice for relief from stings; and for promoting menstruation.

Pearly everlasting
Anaphalis margaritacea Asteraceae

Pearly everlasting is a roadside and open-forest plant with a mass of white blooms from July through August. The stems and undersides of the long, thin dark-green leaves are covered with white wool. Each pearly-white flower head has a yellow-brown centre surrounded by a large number of small parchment-like pastel scales.

The fresh juice is reported to be an aphrodisiac. The plant is useful as a wash and a poultice for external wounds.

Pearly everlasting is often picked in full bloom, dried and used in decorators' winter bouquets.

Pipsissewa
Chimaphila umbellata   Ericaceae

Pipsissewa (or prince's pine) thrives in cool evergreen forests. It is five to 10 inches high, with leathery, dark-green sharply toothed leaves clustered around the stem in loose whorls year-round. The waxy pink-white flowers cluster near the top of the stem in a bunch of three to nine.

Pipsissewa is high in vitamin C and salicin. The root and leaves can be boiled and the liquid allowed to cool for a refreshing tonic. The leaves may be eaten raw and are used as an ingredient for commercial root beer.

The plant's most interesting reported use is as an antibiotic. It has been found to be one of the most active antibiotic plants and is used in the manufacture of some modern medicines.

In its natural form, pipsissewa has been used to treat heart and kidney diseases, rheumatism, gonorrhea, diabetes and skin diseases.

Pipsissewa

Plantain
Plantago spp.   Plantaginaceae

Plantain is a very common, useful plant that prefers open moist ground. It often grows around houses, in old roadways and alongside highways. Plantain leaves are ribbed and smooth, and are piled up around the base of a stem, which is otherwise leafless. The flowers are small, greenish and arranged in dense spikes at the top of the stem.

Young plantain leaves are good raw. Like many other plant leaves, they become quite fibrous as they age. Plantain seeds can be eaten parched or ground into meal.

Plantain is very good for dressing sores, ulcers, wounds, insect bites, snakebites, bee stings, burns, boils and scalds. The fresh leaves can be mashed to a pulp and applied. A strong infusion of plantain is good for quick relief of the external irritation of piles. The seeds act as a laxative when soaked in water and eaten raw. An infusion of the leaves is supposed to be good for kidney and bladder troubles and expelling worms. The roots beaten into a powder are supposed to be good for toothache. The leaves crushed and applied to the forehead help to relieve headache. Applied externally or as an infusion, plantain is generally very effective for all wounds.

The chemical constituents of plantain include a large amount of potassium and calcium, as well as pectin, resin and citric and oxalic acids.

Plantain fibre can be used in making fabric.

Plantain

Prickly pear cactus
Opuntia spp.

Cactaceae

Prickly pear cactus grows in arid desert areas—in the Similkameen, Okanagan and Nicola valleys north to Kamloops; in Clinton, Lytton and dry places on the southern Gulf Islands; and in the Peace River region. Leaves, when present, are small, scale-like and reddish. Flowers are large, waxy and yellow; they first appear in early June. Fruit is a berry about an inch long. The thick, spongy stem carries out the function of leaves; it is flat-jointed and divided into plate-like sections called internodes. Prickly pear cactus has long barbed spines and numerous fine bristles. Each stem is two to five inches high.

The fruit is good, and the pulp of both leaves and stems can be eaten raw or cooked. The easiest way to obtain the pulp is to slice off the ends of a stem and split it lengthwise, then scoop out the pulp. A syrup can be made by boiling down peeled fruit and straining out the seeds. Seeds may be used in soup or dried and ground for flour. All species have edible fruit, but some are too small.

The fleshy pods may be split after soaking for binding wounds and bruises. They are also a good laxative and useful for treating dysentery.

Prickly pear cactus yields a red dye.

Prickly pear cactus
with sage in background

Purslane
Portulaca oleracea, var. *sativa*   Portulacaceae

Purslane has a stout, prostrate stem that is often reddish. Its numerous branches at the base form large circular mats. Leaves are thick, fleshy, hairless, dark shiny green and much grouped at the branch tips. Flowers appear about mid-July; they have five small yellow petals. Flowers are stemless, appearing in the leaf axils or at stem tips. Purslane flowers open only on mornings of sunny days. The plant grows best in the rich soil of cultivated fields, waste places and gardens. It is abundant in the Okanagan.

The entire plant, except for thick stems, can be eaten raw or cooked. It is rich in vitamins and minerals, and higher in iron content than any green except for parsley. It is also high in oxalic acid. If nipped off, the green tops will sprout again.

Purslane seeds are supposed to be good for expelling worms, especially in children. An infusion of purslane is reportedly good for stomachache, excessive menstrual flow and high blood pressure. The juice combined with honey makes a cough medicine substitute.

Rose
Rosa spp.   Rosaceae

Wild roses have pink or white flowers that bloom from May until July. Then the fruit hips ripen. The plants may grow several feet high in shrubs, and they prefer open fields or the edge of forests. Wild roses smell particularly delicious.

Rosehips are a famous source of vitamin C. They can be eaten raw all fall and winter, canned for juice, used for tea, ground for meal or flour, and used in jams and soups. Boiling fresh rosehips is said to extract about 40 percent of the vitamin C; drying is said to extract about 64 percent. Rose petals make a delicately scented tea, and the twigs and roots can be peeled and boiled for tea as well. The petals are supposed to have a mild astringent and tonic effect on the body. The hips are excellent for sore throat, colds, influenza, etc., and the roots are reportedly also useful in those ways.

Oil from the petals can be used as a perfume for a bath or hair rinse, and the dried petals are often used in sachets.

Illustration next page

Rosehip

Sage and wormwood
Artemisia spp.   Asteraceae

Of the many species of *Artemisia* in BC, the most common ones are best. *A. frigida* (wormwood), having fringed leaves, is found throughout the Interior, from Lytton eastward and as far north as Hazelton. *A. tridentata,* recognized by its triple-notched leaves, is common throughout the Interior, as is *A. absinthium.* Sage and wormwood are found in the dry, open soil of valleys and hills to an altitude of 5,000 feet. Leaves are silver-grey and have a characteristic sage odour. The small yellow flowers are in heads and appear at the end of summer. Sages vary from herbaceous plants to large woody shrubs. They are usually three to four feet high but may attain heights of 10 feet.

Sage can be used as a seasoning or an aromatic bitter. Sage tea is soothing and quieting for the nerves.

As medicine, sage and wormwood are good for teething pain, sore throat, colds, asthma, influenza and toothache; as a tooth cleanser and for producing strong circulation. Boiled sage or wormwood leaves are useful in a bath for rheumatism, aches and pains. Because sage and wormwood are highly astringent, they are useful as a powder, wash or poultice for sores and wounds. Throat and chest congestion can be relieved by inhaling the fumes, drinking the tea or having a poultice applied directly to the skin. Oil from the flowers is poisonous to insects and intestinal worms.

Sage is excellent as a hair tonic or shampoo. Sage and wormwood are effective as a moth and flea repellent.

Illustrations next page

Sage

Wormwood

INWOOD '72

St. John's wort or Klamath weed
Hypericum perforatum   Hypericaceae

St. John's wort is a perennial found at low elevations across BC from Vancouver Island to the Kootenays, but most extensively in the lower Fraser Valley and around New Westminster, Vancouver and Victoria. It prefers sandy, gravelly, poor dry soil. Its stemless, opposite leaves have small transparent dots that can be seen when the leaves are held up to the light. By the end of June, the plant has many yellow flowers with five petals that have black dots around the edges. The stem is one to three feet high, much branched, rust-coloured and hairless. It is woody at the base and green above. The seed pod is rusty brown and about a quarter of an inch long.

St. John's wort is reportedly excellent in internal infusion for chronic uterine troubles, after-pain in childbirth, promotion of menstruation, and bedwetting. Used externally as an ointment or poultice, it is supposed to be good on bruises, scratches, bites, scalds, skin eruptions and blisters.

St. John's wort contains a phytotoxin called hypericin that can cause photosensitivity (of skin to light), with the result that the skin forms lesions. It causes severe irritation and weight loss for white-furred animals when they're exposed to strong sunlight after eating the plant.

Illustration next page

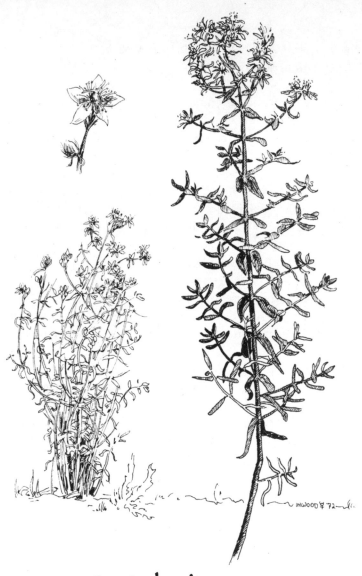

St. John's wort

Salsify
Tragopogon spp.

Asteraceae

Salsify (or oyster plant) is a common wildflower in fields and meadows in the BC Interior. It is widely cultivated in other places. It has a bright yellow, dandelion-like flower that is replaced by a big, round seed head by July. Leaves are alternate, clasping and grass-like.

The young stem and leaves and the thick root of salsify can be eaten raw or boiled.

Salsify

Sarsaparilla
Aralia nudicaulis   Araliaceae

Wild sarsaparilla is found along the floor of semi-open and open forests and is easily identifiable, with a short stem branching into three arms, each carrying three to five oval leaflets two to four inches long. The umbrella cluster of tiny white-green flowers is usually hidden from sight by the leaves. Plump greenish-brown inedible seeds grow in the fall.

The sarsaparilla found in BC has properties similar to but milder than those of the tropical species. A tea made from the root gathered in the autumn is delicious. It has been used elsewhere as an ingredient for soft drinks and as a commercial beverage by itself.

Medicinally, a sarsaparilla infusion is used as a tonic for increasing appetite and purifying the blood. It can also serve as a remedy for internal inflammation, fevers, rheumatism and skin eruptions. The infusion can be used as an eyewash or an antidote for poisons. There are no harmful effects from sarsaparilla, so it can be consumed freely.

INWOOD ♀ '71

Sarsaparilla

Shepherd's purse
Capsella bursa-pastoris   Brassicaceae

Shepherd's purse is one of those garden weeds that can be as valuable as the cultivated plants themselves. It grows in dry, open ground and gets its name from the purse-shaped seed pods along the stem. There is a circle of dandelion-like leaves at the base, and the flowers, in terminal clusters, are small and usually white.

Young leaves have a pleasant peppery taste when eaten raw. Seeds can be cooked and ground for meal, while roots can be used as a substitute for ginger.

Besides containing large amounts of vitamins A and C, calcium, sulphur and sodium, shepherd's purse is extremely high in vitamin K—the blood-clotting vitamin. Infusions are excellent for internal hemorrhaging of all kinds, including excessive menstruation. Poultices and ointments serve equally well for external wounds. Shepherd's purse is also recommended for intermittent fevers and rheumatic afflictions, hemorrhoids and diarrhea.

Shepherd's purse

Skullcap
Scutellaria spp.   Lamiaceae

The species of skullcap we commonly see (*S. galericulata*) grows in marshy ground near rivers and streams with some other members of the mint family. It has the characteristic square stem and opposite toothed leaves, but the flowers are blue and in pairs. The most distinguishing feature of skullcap is a little skullcap projection or crest on the calyx where the flower begins. Flowers bloom in July and August.

Medicinally, skullcap has been used for convulsions, headaches, and pain from coughs and hiccuping. We find the tea relaxing and conducive to sleep. Signs of overdose are said to be giddiness, stupor, confusion, and twitching of the limbs.

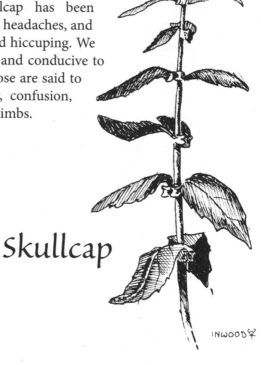

Skullcap

INWOOD♀

Snowbrush
Ceanothus velutinus   Rhamnaceae

Snowbrush (or mountain balm) is a brushy, sprawling shrub found alongside old roads in the BC Interior. Its thick evergreen leaves are about two inches long, glossy and gummy on the top surface, and soft and velvety on the underside, and have three main veins. When the summer heat becomes intense, the leaves curl lengthwise along their centre to prevent water loss. The flowers are clusters of tiny, white, soft buds that later turn to small, hard husks. They bloom in June and July. Both the leaves and the flowers have a strong, pleasant fragrance.

The flowers make a soapy lather with warm water and feel nice on the skin and hair. The leaves have been used along with other herbs like kinnikinnick for smoking. The leaves and flowers are said to make a stimulating tea that's good for stomach and liver disorders. An infusion of the root and root bark may relieve internal bleeding, serve as an astringent and relieve irritability.

Snowbrush contains saponins—poisonous glycosides, so it's important to consume only small amounts

Sorrel
Sheep sorrel (*Rumex crispus*)   Polygonaceae
Mountain sorrel (*Rumex acetosella*)

Curled dock
Oxyria spp.   Polygonaceae

Both sorrels have a slender stalk less than a foot high; curled dock grows to three feet. Greenish flowers give rise to conspicuous reddish-brown fruit in all three plants. Curled dock leaves curl at the edges; sheep sorrel leaves are long-pointed with a curved edge; mountain sorrel leaves are round or kidney-shaped. Sheep sorrel and curled dock are found in the valley fields and waysides in poor, exposed soil. Mountain sorrel is found on higher rocky slopes.

The sorrels and dock can be distinguished from other plants by their pleasantly sour-tasting leaves. These leaves are good as seasoning for salads, soups and egg dishes. They can also be used for a sort of rhubarb pie, jam, and a cooling beverage. All three plants and related species are rich in vitamins A and C but should be eaten sparingly because of their high oxalic acid content.

Medicinally, sorrel and dock leaves are used in juice or tea form to treat urinary and kidney diseases, cool a fever or quench thirst, expel worms, increase the appetite or purify the blood. Dock root serves as a laxative. Boiled in wine, sorrel is reportedly a good remedy for abdominal pain. All three plants are also recommended for dispelling itching from insect bites, nettle sting, snakebite, etc.

Speedwell or brooklime
Veronica spp.   Plantaginaceae

Speedwell has opposite, oval, hairy leaves, a roundish stem and small wheel-shaped flowers that are usually white or blue. Flowers have two stamens and two pairs of opposite petals, one pair of which is unequal-sized. They first appear around early June. Each of the flat, heart-shaped seed capsules contains many seeds. The plant reaches a height of about three feet and is found in moist, open areas from low to subalpine elevations.

Watercress and mint are often nearby.

The leaves and stems, especially the upper portions, are edible raw or cooked but are bitter raw after the plant is in flower. Speedwell is high in vitamin C. It is mild and succulent, with a slight pungency.

As medicine, speedwell removes mucus: it is good for coughs, catarrh and asthma.

Roots can be divided and replanted.

Spring beauty
Claytonia lanceolata   Portulacaceae

Spring beauty is a tiny perennial plant. It is one of the first flowers to appear in spring and continues to grow in moist places all summer. The base of the stem is thickened into an edible bulb. There is one pair of opposite, narrow, lance-shaped leaves, and the flowers are small and pinkish-white.

The leaves and flowers are delicious raw, and the starchy bulb can be eaten raw, boiled or roasted like a potato. It is said to preserve well when cooked and mashed into cakes for drying.

Stonecrop
Sedum spp.   Crassulaceae

The variety of stonecrop we commonly see is a rock plant with bright yellow, star-like flowers rising on a thick stalk from fleshy leaves arranged like a cactus rosette. Other species have white or rose-coloured flowers and are called orpine and life everlasting.

The young stems and leaves of stonecrop can be eaten raw or as a pot-herb. As the leaves mature, they take on a rather bitter taste and may produce slight nausea.

Stonecrop is reportedly mucilaginous and slightly astringent, of value in the treatment of ulcers, wounds, lung disorders and diarrhea.

Stonecrop

Spring beauty

Strawberry blite or blite goosefoot
Chenopodium capitatum   Amaranthaceae

Strawberry blite has large but thin triangular green leaves; they may be six inches long and are formed alternately on a thick-ridged stem. Flowers are greenish, small and inconspicuous. The plant takes its name from the bright red strawberry-like fruit that forms in small, round clusters at intervals along the stem in early fall. It is common across BC, especially on stony or upturned ground, but is most abundant in northern areas of the province.

The "strawberries" are edible raw or cooked, and the leaves can be cooked as greens. Like lamb's quarters, strawberry blite contains oil of chenopodium, which can be toxic in large amounts. The related plant wormseed (*Chenopodium ambrosioides anthelminticum*) is much used as a remedy for intestinal worms.

Sunflower
Helianthus annuus and other spp.   Asteraceae

Sunflowers are found in low-altitude meadows and water-courses. Ray flowers are yellow but disc flowers can be yellow, purple or brown depending on the species. (Flower heads in the Compositae family usually have two kinds of flowers composing the blossom: tubular flowers on the large central disc and a ring of flattened, petal-like ray flowers surrounding them.) Sunflower heads are on the top of coarse stems that can grow to 10 feet; they are large, showy and either solitary or in small bunches. Leaves are stalkless, and seeds are flattened and sometimes four-sided.

Sunflower seeds can be eaten raw or roasted, or ground into meal. They are very high in protein (50 percent), natural fats (35 percent), vitamin B and minerals. Oil is extracted by boiling crushed seeds and skimming the oil from the surface of the cooled liquid. Both shells and seeds can be roasted and used as a coffee substitute. Jerusalem artichoke (*Helianthus tuberosus*) is a sunflower with large edible tubers.

Sunflower seeds yield a bland fixing oil that can be used in soap making and candle making, as a lubricant and as hair oil. Flowers yield a yellow dye.

Thistle
Cirsium spp.

Asteraceae

Several species of this common weed grow in BC. Some are short and others are over six feet tall. Leaves are usually lobed, ending in sharp spines, and the flowers cluster in spiny, burr-like heads that are usually purple, white or reddish.

The young plant stem can be peeled and eaten raw or used as a pot-herb, while the young leaves can be used as a tea. The root can be peeled and eaten raw, boiled or roasted, and the fruitlike seeds can be eaten raw or roasted.

Medicinally, thistle infusions are good for aiding stomach conditions, reducing fever, getting rid of worms, and increasing the milk supply in nursing mothers.

Thistledown makes excellent tinder.

Thistle

Valerian
Valeriana sitchensis   Caprifoliaceae

Valerian is a common subalpine perennial seen as soon as the snow recedes. The flowers are fragrant and pinkish-white, the leaves are opposite and coarsely toothed, and the root is tuberous and odiferous.

Eaten raw, valerian root is reportedly poisonous, but if cooked for a long time, nutritious.

The plant is used as a sedative to reduce pain and promote sleep. It is said to slow the heart while increasing its strength and is valuable for use in treating mental stress-induced nervousness because of having no known narcotic side effects. Valerian root is also used to improve eyesight when the optic nerve is weak and as a remedy for coughing (boiled with licorice root and raisins). It has a soothing, tonic effect when added to a bath. The tea seems to us to slow down and relax our bodies and produce a deep, restful sleep.

Valerian flower's fragrance has been used to scent ointments.

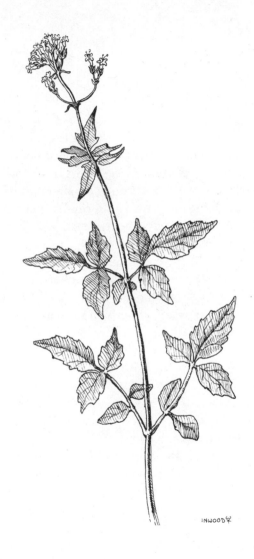

Valerian

Vanilla leaf
Achlys triphylla   Berberidaceae

Woodruff
Asperula odorata   Rubiaceae

We like these two plants for their similar fragrances.

Vanilla leaf covers large areas of the forest floor at low and middle elevations west of the Cascades. A thin foot-high stem holds a single leaf that is beautifully divided into three wavy-edged leaflets, giving the plant a butterfly-like appearance. The thin flower stem rising above the leaflets in May has a spike of small white flowers.

Woodruff is a small, creeping, vine-like perennial found on shaded forest floors throughout southern BC. Its narrow leaves grow in successive star-like whorls, each containing six to eight leaflets. Stems are smooth and usually trail along the ground. Fine stalks with small white flowers appear just above the leaves in June. The flowers are later replaced by small, rough seed balls covered with hooked bristles. (Cleavers/goosegrass—*Galium aparine*—with which woodruff is often confused, also has leaves in whorls of six to eight and small white flowers clustered in the upper leaf axils, but cleavers is a more erect plant and has a hairy, sticky stem.)

Both plants contain coumarin, which is responsible for the vanilla-like odour when they are dried. This odour supposedly repels flies; some authors recommend hanging a bunch of dried leaves in a room. We do so for their fine aroma.

Woodruff (and cleavers) is recommended in infusion form for all kinds of fever and to increase lactation.

Watercress
Nasturtium spp. Brassicaceae

This famous edible plant grows in or along streambeds. The stalk is slender, with branches of succulent oval-pointed leaves, several opposite and one on the end. The flowers are white.

The leaves, flowers and seeds are rich in vitamins A, C, D and E, as well as calcium and the trace elements. These parts can be used raw, in teas, as a pot-herb, or dried to flavour food with their characteristic peppery taste. The underwater parts or roots should be discarded, as they tend to be tough and unpalatable.

Watercress is valued medicinally for its antiscorbutic (anti-scurvy) qualities and for treating colds and sinus troubles and is best used when in flower. The juice or bruised leaves reportedly rid the face of spots and blemishes. Watercress contains fluorine, iron, sodium, sulphur, potassium, phosphorous and magnesium.

Yarrow
Achillea millefolium   Asteraceae

Yarrow is found in almost any exposed area. It is a strongly scented perennial, usually under two feet high. The leaves are divided into numerous narrow divisions resembling large, fuzzy pipe cleaners along the hairy stem. White flowers bloom most of the summer on the top of the stalk in small, numerous heads, which together form a dense, flat-topped arrangement.

Yarrow makes a nourishing tea or broth. It is a strong astringent and tonic that is excellent when applied to bleeding wounds, inflammation and rashes. It is good for colds, sore throat, hiccuping and fever. It soothes and heals sore mucous membranes and hemorrhaging and bleeding from the lungs. Yarrow is also reportedly good for bleeding piles, excessive menstruation, eruptive diseases like measles, diarrhea in infants, worms, cramps and kidney disorders. It can be used as a local anaesthetic and a disinfectant; chewing the leaves is one of the best ways we know to relieve toothache. An infusion of the leaves makes an excellent hair tonic.

Yarrow

We've left out many fine food and medicinal plants. Some are far more beautiful than useful; others are either not very common or too easily confused with poisonous plants. You may want to consult other sources of information about the following:

Angelica (*Angelica* spp.)

Arnica (*Arnica* spp.)

Ballhead waterleaf (*Hydrophyllum capitatum*)

Bistort (*Polygonum bistortoides*)

Brodiaea (*Brodiaea douglasii*)

Carrot leaf (*Leptotaenia dissecta*)

Cow parsnip (*Heracleum lanatum*)

Evening primrose (*Oenothera biennis, hookeri*)

Filaree (*Erodium cicutarium*)

Licorice (*Glycyrrhiza lepidota*)

Lilies (*Liliaceae*)

Queen Anne's lace (*Daucus carota*)

Sedges (*Carex* spp.)

Shooting star (*Dodecatheon* spp.)

Trillium (*Trillium* spp.)

Wild caraway (*Carum gairdneri* or *Perideridia gairdneri*)

Yellow bell (*Fritillaria pudica*)

Berries

Berries are seeds wrapped in juices and pulp. They are found throughout southern BC except for salal, which is only found near the coast and around Kootenay Lake.

Edible berries can be eaten raw, boiled into syrup, squeezed for juice, cooked with other foods, dried or made into cakes. Young shoots of several species, particularly salmonberry, blackberry, thimbleberry and blackcap, are excellent as greens in the spring. Tea made from berry leaves is delicious.

Several of the berry-producing plants are used medicinally. Blueberries are considered cooling to the liver and stomach. An eyewash can be made from the boiled green inner bark of serviceberries. Salmonberry bark can be pounded and applied to an aching tooth or festering wound to relieve pain. Blackberry roots and berries contain the astringents gallic acid and tannin, and are good for treating diarrhea. The best effect is obtained from eating many of the berries or drinking a decocted tea. Blackberry leaves are useful for burns, and the leaves and flowers have been used for snakebite.

Some of the most delicious berries are described below. Also, see descriptions of Oregon grape, elder, wild rose, strawberry blite and kinnikinnick.

Wild blackberry

Wild raspberry

Wild strawberry

Ericaceae

Huckleberries and blueberries (*Vaccinium* spp.) are red, blue or blue-black berries that grow on an upright shrub without prickles on the stems. Leaves are single and minutely lobed in some varieties.

Cranberries (*Vaccinium* spp.) are red, single berries found on a trailing or climbing vine. Leaves are single and untoothed. The plant is most often found in bogs.

Salal (*Gaultheria shallon*) has dull purple or blue, hairy berries in stemmed clusters. It is an upright shrub without prickles on its sticky stalks. Leaves are stiff, thick and single with finely toothed margins.

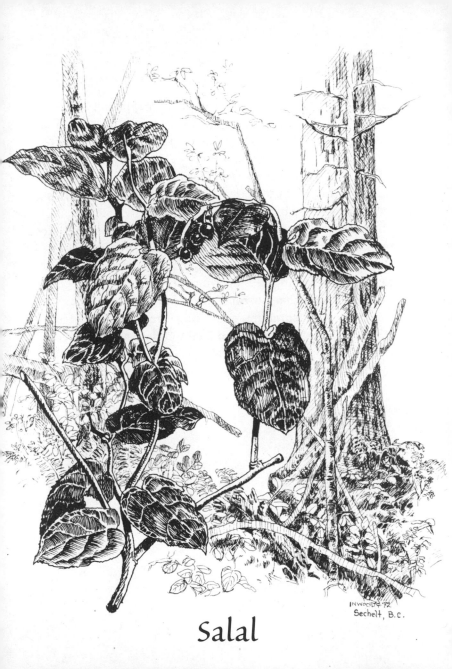

Salal

Rosaceae

Serviceberries or Juneberries (*Amelanchier* spp.) are smooth, dull purplish-blue berries found in stemmed clusters. The plant is an upright shrub without prickles. Leaves are single, thin, papery-soft and finely toothed.

Thimbleberries (*Rubus parviflorus*) are dull red berries found in stemmed clusters on an upright shrub without prickles. Leaves are very broad, maple-like, lobed and hairy.

Salmonberries, raspberries and blackcaps (*Rubus* spp.) are orange, red and reddish-black fruits with many seeds. These plants are also upright and lacking prickles on the stems. Leaves are divided into leaflets from a central stalk.

Blackberries (*Rubus ursinus*) are red to black berries found on a trailing or climbing vine. They are compound fruits with many seeds; leaves are divided into leaflets from a central point.

Wild strawberries (*Fragaria glauca*) are red compound berries having many seeds and are found on a soft-stemmed annual herb. Leaves are divided into leaflets that are bluish and hairy.

Salmonberry

Saxifragaceae

Wild gooseberries (*Ribes* spp.) are red to dark red or black-ish berries. The plant is an upright shrub with prickles on the stem, compound fruit with many seeds, and leaves under four inches long divided into leaflets from a central point.

Currants (*Ribes* spp.) are single reddish, dull purple or blue berries found on an upright shrub without prickles. Leaves are lobed or divided into leaflets from a central point.

Wild gooseberry

Seaweeds

Attached marine algae, or seaweeds, are characteristic of the beach between low- and high-tide lines. About 500 species of seaweed have been identified along the 17,000 miles of the BC coast. Many of these are difficult to identify, even for specialists. About 30 of them are used as food in other countries.

Most seaweeds are a poor source of food in their natural form because much of the plant material is indigestible and too high in inorganic substances. Drying and powdering or cooking helps. No poisonous seaweed is known, although some are more palatable than others. Polluted water should be avoided when gathering seaweeds. Seaweeds produce little heat when digested and assimilated, so they are good hot-weather foods. They are rich in vitamins B and C and extremely high in most minerals, especially iodine, iron, potassium and sodium. All seaweeds can be dried, ground and used for seasoning food. Some seaweeds taste peppery, others slightly sweet. A bread can be made of seaweed meal and wheat flour. Seaweeds can be boiled with milk and flour, fried alone or with fish, used as a gelatin for fixing puddings and aspic-like salads, used for steaming clams, and stuffed with rice. Tender seaweeds can be nibbled raw, especially dulse. Cakes can be made by pressing seaweed into blocks, drying and slicing it as needed. Soak dried seaweed in fresh water before using it in soups, steeping as a drink, or whipping to a froth to serve with berries or other fruit. Seaweeds have been used as an ingredient for alcoholic beverages.

Seaweeds are useful as a wound dressing because of their high absorbency and iodine content. They are also useful as fertilizer and for cleaning utensils.

A few of the most abundant and widely used seaweeds are described below.

Pacific kelp

Brown algae

The kelps (*Alaria* spp., *Nereocystis luetkeana* and *Macrocystis integrifolia*) are brown annuals with a stalk (sometimes 100 feet long) anchored to the ocean bottom by a root-like holdfast and expanding into a hollow bulb at the top. Two pairs of long, leaf-like fronds are attached to the bulb. Kelp grows in water that's five to 50 feet deep.

Bladderwrack, seawrack or rockweed (*Fucus gardneri*) is a very common olive-green to dark-brown weed attached to rocks along the beach. It is rigid and cartilaginous, is up to a foot long, and has many flattened branches that are swollen at the tips. These bladders are filled with gas and a buoyant mucilaginous material.

Green algae

Sea lettuce (*Ulva lactuca*) is formed of very thin, translucent sheets or ribbons that are bright green. It is often ruffled along the margins and split into broad lobes tapering abruptly near the base. It is found on rocks near the high-tide line or in mud flats in quiet bays and lagoons.

Bladderwrack

Red algae

Red laver (*Porphyra perforata*) sometimes looks like a thin, delicate, red sea lettuce. It consists of single thin membranes up to five feet long forming broad, irregular lobes of deeply ruffled margins attached by a small, disc-like holdfast.

Agar (*Ahnfeltia* spp.) is deep red to purplish-black, erect and up to a foot long, and grows in dense tufts attached by a disc-like holdfast. It is wiry and stiff, with branches that are sometimes densely tangled.

Dulse (*Rhodymenia* spp.) is a brownish-red to reddish-purple erect seaweed usually found in clusters; it is attached similarly to red laver and agar. Its broad, flat blade, one to two feet long, is divided in two.

All three of these red algae attach themselves to rocks and other algae in the lower intertidal zone at a depth of about 100 feet.

Trees

Alder

Mountain alder (*Alnus tenuifolia*)   Betulaceae
Red alder (*Alnus rubra*)
Sitka alder (*Alnus sinuata*)

Red and sitka alder grow along the BC coast. Sitka alder is found as far inland as the Cascades. Mountain alder grows in the mountainous regions of the Interior. All three prefer damp soil. Sitka alder is shrub-like; the others reach 50 feet. All alder leaves are oval and toothed, forming alternately on the stem. Tassel-like catkins appear in early spring before the leaves. Male and female flowers are found on the same tree. Leaf buds are mostly stalked. Seeds are in small woody cones. Leaves remain green in the fall. Bark is grey-green, smooth on young trees, scaly on older ones. Long, horizontal lenticels mark the bark.

Alder buds and the young inner bark are edible.

A decoction of the leaves is useful for burns and inflamed wounds. Fresh leaves can be placed in shoes to provide relief to tired, aching feet; they also reduce swelling and keep feet cool. Dew-moistened leaves reportedly banish fleas from their immediate area.

As a poultice, pulped leaves moistened with warm milk relieve external swellings and inflammation. Alder bark contains much tannin and is a strong astringent. It is useful in decoction for diarrhea, upset stomach and hemorrhage, as eye drops, for colds and sore throat and as an ointment for eruptive skin diseases.

In arid regions, alder indicates the presence of water. Red, brown or black dyes can be extracted from the bark. The wood is soft and fine-grained; it works easily and stains well.

If cut and seasoned, it won't split in the sun. Alder makes excellent fuel because it doesn't throw sparks and leaves little ash.

Birch

Water birch (*Betula occidentalis*)   Betulaceae
White or paper birch (*Betula papyrifera,* var. *occidentalis*)

Paper birch grows throughout BC, especially in burned-over areas and at the edge of clearings in well-drained, sandy soil. Water birch is usually found near streams or springs in the Interior. Both have alternate, rounded leaves with pointed ends, are toothed and light green. The underside is often finely dotted. Buds are stalkless and pointed. Male and female flowers are found on the same tree. Paper birch bark peels readily from older trees but disfigures the tree for years. Lenticels prominently mark the bark. Water birch usually remains shrubby; white birch may reach 80 feet.

Birch is rich in vitamins and minerals. The red inner bark is aromatic either fresh or dried and is good added to soups and stews. A tea can be made from the leaves and the sap used like maple syrup. Commercially, wintergreen is obtained from some birches as a flavouring for medicine, candy, etc.

Birch buds and leaves can be used as a salve for arthritis and rheumatism; methyl salicylate is the active ingredient. A strong bark decoction dissolves kidney stones, and a milder solution is good for sore throat. Sap or juice from the young leaves is effective in treating external skin irritations and scurvy.

Birch

Cedar

Western red cedar (*Thuja plicata*)   Pinaceae
Yellow cedar or Nootka false cypress (*Chamaecyparis noot-katensis*)

Western red cedar grows throughout southern BC, yellow cedar only along the coast. Both prefer rich, moist soil. Cedars have scaly, blunt needles pressed in pairs tightly to the twig. Yellow cedar needles are prickly to the touch when stroked backwards. Cedar limbs sweep downward and the trunk tapers from a fluted base. Male and female organs are on the same tree in small separate cones; female cones are spherical. Cedar bark is thin and stringy—dark on red cedar and light on yellow cedar. Old trees often have dead branches in the crown and dense foliage. Cedars are long-lived, slow-growing trees, sometimes living for 800 years. Red cedar may reach 150 feet, yellow cedar only 80 feet.

Cedar buds can be chewed for toothache. An infusion of the bark and twigs is good for kidney troubles and a decoction of fruit and leaves for coughs. Steam from such an infusion was inhaled by First Nations peoples to promote delivery in childbirth, along with hard pressure and kneading of the abdomen.

Cedar wood is resistant to rot and insect decay. Red cedar is especially fine for building boats and houses, and makes easily wrought shingles and fence posts. Rope and thread for weaving can be made from the inner bark. First, separate the bark into long strips, removing the woody outer layer. Then, boil in water with sifted wood ashes to soften the fibre. Remove, dry and separate into small filaments by pounding along the grain. Remove any remaining wood splinters by pulling fibres over a ridged surface. Boil before using to make the fibres supple.

Cedar

Cherry

Bitter cherry (*Prunus emarginata*)   Rosaceae
Pin cherry (*Prunus pensylvanica*)
Western chokecherry (*Prunus virginiana*, var. *demissa*)

Bitter cherry is found in southern BC in moist regions, especially along streams and bordering wooded areas. Pin cherry
and chokecherry are found in rich soils in open places and
along streams in the Interior. These are usually shrub-like but
may grow to 25 feet. Bitter cherry can grow to 40 feet. Pin cherry
has lance-shaped leaves; the others have more oval leaves. All
are sharp-pointed and finely toothed. The flowers are white
and grow in fragrant, erect clusters, blooming just as the leaves
appear. The fruit has juicy flesh and a single stone. The bark has a
bitter taste and odour. It is grey-brown to red-brown with greyish
lenticels. Male and female parts are found on the same flowers.

Cherries are edible although they tend to be sour. They are
good as jelly or syrup, or added to other foods. The young shoots
and bark can be used as a cooked vegetable. Hydrocyanic acid is
found in the pits and leaves, but cooking removes it from leaves.
Pits should be discarded.

An infusion or syrup of the bark can be used as a sedative.
Tea made from bark shavings is good for coughs and loosening
phlegm. Smoking pulverized bark is effective for headache and
head colds. Inhaling the steam from boiling bark is said to cure
snow blindness. Pulverized dried bark is also good for sores,
sexually transmitted diseases, diarrhea and nervousness. The
fruit is also a good remedy for diarrhea. Chokecherry juice was
consumed by First Nations people to stop postpartum hemorrhages. A decoction of chokecherry gum, powdered mallow
root and skullcap was drunk to eliminate afterbirth.

Fir

Douglas fir (*Pseudotsuga taxifolia*)   Pinaceae

Douglas fir is found throughout southern BC. Along the coast it is usually tall and straight, in the Interior, stockier and shorter, with blue-green foliage. The tree has a strong root system resistant to wind damage, and occasionally lives for a thousand years. Cones are pendant with three-pointed bracts extending beyond the end of each scale. Leaf scars are small and raised. (True firs have upright cones without bracts and larger, depressed leaf scars.) Buds are pointed, dry and brown. Old trees frequently have few branches.

The needles are rich in vitamin C and good as tea.

As medicine, a decoction of twigs is useful for colds. A bark decoction is a laxative.

Pitch can be applied directly to cuts, boils and sores or made into a poultice.

Alpine fir (*Abies lasiocarpa*)
Cascades fir or Pacific silver fir (*Abies amabilis*)
Grand fir (*Abies grandis*)

True firs are similar to Douglas fir, except for the above-noted differences, and that buds are rounded and dry or resinous. Grand fir is found in low-altitude rich forests, Cascades fir on the coast and in subalpine regions of the Interior, and alpine fir near the timberline.

As with Douglas fir, the needles are rich in vitamin C.

A decoction of the twigs is useful for colds. Pitch can be applied externally to cuts, boils and sores.

Hazel
Hazel or filbert (*Corylus* spp.)   Betulaceae

Hazel is a small bushy tree found in rocky or moist soil in
central BC and the wetter areas of the coast, especially near
Victoria. Leaves are toothed and oval with a pointed tip.
Yellow catkins hang from the twigs just before spring. Husks
are bristly and green. Nuts are brown and oval, pointed at one
end and flat at the other.

Hazelnuts can be eaten raw, roasted or ground for meal.
Watch the squirrels: you'll be able to tell when the hazelnuts
are ripe.

Hemlock

Mountain hemlock (*Tsuga mertensiana*)   Pinaceae
Western hemlock (*Tsuga heterophylla*)

Western hemlock is found along the coast and in the wet Interior. Mountain hemlock is found near the timberline in southern BC. The needles of western hemlock are mostly two-ranked, flattened, grooved, lustrous, dark green above and marked with two broad white bands below. Mountain hemlock needles are tufted or rounded toward the upper side, flattened or grooved above, and rounded or ribbed below; they are pale bluish-green with white bands, both above and below. Mountain hemlock tends to be shrubby near the timberline. Hemlocks have stalked, half-inch needles, flat and blunt-tipped. They are tolerant of shade and have heavy foliage with an irregular crown and a distinctive fragrance. The bark is dark brown with flat, scaly ridges and deep furrows on mature trees. Male and female flowers are found in separate cones on the same tree.

As food, hemlocks are rich in vitamin C. The young shoots can be nibbled raw or used as tea.

An infusion of hemlock is useful as a wash for sore eyes or skin sores. The oil can be used as a liniment for rheumatism. The bark is high in tannin and is a powerful astringent. It can be chewed and applied to hemorrhages or used in decoction for kidney and bladder ailments. The pitch cools and reduces sunburn and prevents chapping. Powdered hemlock can be put into shoes or socks for sore, tender or sweaty feet. Chips or sap accidentally rubbed into cuts can produce hives.

Salve from the gum can be used as a strengthening plaster and as face paint. The bark serves as a red-brown dye and is used in tanning hides.

Juniper
Common juniper (*Juniperus communis*)   Cypress
Rocky Mountain juniper (*Juniperus scopulorum*)

Common juniper is an upright shrub growing in mountainous regions and canyon bottoms. Its needles are prickly, less than half an inch long and in whorls of three. Rocky Mountain juniper is a small tree found in the Interior mountains. Its needles are scale-like and in alternate pairs. Junipers have male and female cones on separate trees and grow in rocky soil. The semi-fleshy bluish cones or berries take three years to mature. Juniper bark is reddish grey or brown, thin and fibrous.

Juniper berries can be used in tea or as seasoning for other foods. Common juniper oil is used for flavouring gin.

A tea made from the twigs is said to promote muscular relaxation before childbirth when used every morning. A wash for all types of bites and stings can be made from the decocted berries. A decoction from the berries and twigs is said to be good for reducing fevers, for head colds, in hot packs for rheumatism, and for chronic urogenital disorders and stomach ailments.

Pine

Lodgepole pine (*Pinus contorta*) Pinaceae
Ponderosa pine (*Pinus ponderosa*)
Shore pine (*Pinus contorta latifolia*)
Western white pine (*Pinus monticola*)
Whitebark pine (*Pinus albicaulis*)

Western white pine is found along the coast and in the valleys and slopes of the wet Interior of BC. Its needles, in groups of five, are two to four inches long, and its cones are four to 10 inches long. Whitebark pine is an alpine tree found above 3,000 feet on the coast and above 6,000 feet inland. It can grow on rock faces and cliffs. Its needles are like those of western white pine, but the cones are about an inch smaller. Ponderosa pine is found throughout the southern Interior in moist or dry soils. Its five-to-11-inch needles are in threes, and its cones are three to six inches long. Lodgepole pine is widespread, from sand dunes to swamps to stony ridges, and it is tall and slender. Shore pine on the coast tends to be short and scrubby. Both lodgepole and shore pine needles are one to three inches long, spirally twisted and in twos; cones are one to two inches long. All the pines have separate male and female cones on the same tree.

As food, pine needles contain a high proportion of vitamin A and about five times as much vitamin C as lemons. They can be nibbled or used as tea or food seasoning. Pine seeds are rich in fat and protein; eaten raw, they can be somewhat toxic. Nuts can be pounded into cakes, cooked or used in soup, or made into nut butter. The inner bark can be mashed to a pulp and made into cakes.

As medicine, pine resin is useful for ointments, plasters, cough syrup, and treating burns and sores. The inner bark can be boiled and beaten to a pulp for a poultice or used in strips as bandages, especially for burns and scalds. Charcoal made from nut meats is also said to be useful crushed and applied to sores and burns. Pine gum can be used to draw out infections and slivers. The hardened sap can be dissolved for an eyewash. Buds can be chewed to relieve sore throat. A decoction of the bark is said to be good for stomach disorders. A decoction made from the shoots is used for rheumatism, kidney troubles, boils and coughs.

Ponderosa pine

with kinnikinnick in foreground

Poplar

Black cottonwood (*Populus trichocarpa*)   Salicaceae
Quaking aspen (*Populus tremuloides*)
Tacamahaca poplar (*Populus tacamahaca*)

The three poplars found in BC are most often in well-drained, sandy soil. Black cottonwood is found along the coast and as far inland as the Cascades; Tacamahaca poplar is widespread except for on the coast and in southern BC. Quaking aspen is found in all areas but the southern Rockies. The leaves of black cottonwood and Tacamahaca poplar are about five inches long, tapering from a broad, rounded base. Quaking aspen leaves are nearly circular and up to three inches in diameter. Leaves of all species are light green or whitish below and darker on top with rounded teeth at the edges. Buds are resinous and fragrant. Flowers are small; only one sex is found on a single tree. Bark is yellow to grey-green, smooth on young trees but becoming fissured with age. Poplars are fast-growing and short-lived.

The sap from these species may be drunk directly or boiled down. The inner bark is edible.

A decoction of the bark may be used as a sore-throat gargle. First Nations groups used a syrup made from the bark for setting fractures. They simmered the bark for 24 hours in a large tub, strained the liquid and recooked it to the consistency of honey. After a bone was set, the thick syrup was spread on a cloth, which was wrapped tightly around the fracture. The syrup hardened into a splint. The inner bark of poplars yields a quinine substitute. Stickiness from the buds can be used as an ointment for cuts or as glue.

Poplar wood is light and useful for making small woodenware and furniture.

Black cottonwood (left)
and spruce (right)

Spruce

Black spruce (*Picea mariana*)   Pinaceae
Englemann spruce (*Picea engelmannii*)
Sitka spruce (*Picea sitchensis*)
White spruce (*Picea glauca*)

White spruce grows along the shores of streams and lakes throughout inland BC. Engelmann spruce grows in rich, moist soil at high elevations. Sitka spruce grows in a narrow strip along the coast at low elevations. Black spruce may be found in northern inland bogs. Sitka spruce has two-sided needles; the others have four-sided needles. Black spruce has half-inch needles that are rigid but not prickly. Other species have prickly needles twice as long. All spruce needles grow from woody, peg-like bases. Trunks are long and straight, ending in characteristically dense and spire-like crowns. Male and female cones are found on the same tree. Sitka spruce may grow to 200 feet, white and Engelmann to 100 feet, and black to 40 feet.

Young spruce shoots are aromatic. They are good nibbled or as tea, especially with lemon and honey.

Spruce gum can be applied to cuts and wounds and used as a plaster for setting bones. A decoction from the twigs is good in baths, for colds and for loosening catarrh. The gum is also used on the face to protect against sunburn.

Illustration previous page

Willow
Willow (*Salix* spp.)   Salicaceae

There are many species of willow, all difficult to differentiate from each other. Willows are usually found near water. Male and female flowers are on different trees. Leaves are alternate, dark green above and white below, and long, thin and finely toothed. Twigs are long and pliable. There are often several trunks at the base. Most willows are shrubs, but some become trees. The bark has a bitter taste and is often brightly coloured, especially in winter.

Young leaves and peeled shoots are edible raw. The inner bark can be eaten raw but is better dried and ground into flour.

A decoction of the inner bark, rich in salicylic acid, is an excellent aspirin substitute. First Nations used a bark infusion for venereal disease, and bruised leaves as an astringent on cuts and wounds. Willow is also used as a substitute for quinine.

Poisonous Plants

This section describes the important poisonous plants in BC. While their number might seem considerable, there is probably more danger from cultivated plants and vegetables (tomato leaves, rhubarb leaves, potato sprouts, apple seeds and cherry pits) than from most of these. Any plants that are bitter or unpalatable should be avoided. Any parsley-like plants should be avoided if identification is uncertain. Of these poisonous plants, the most dangerous is probably death camas, which can easily be mistaken for camas and wild onion, and water hemlock, which has succulent-looking leaves in spring. There are few poisonous berries, though many unpalatable ones: baneberry, poison ivy and poison oak have white berries; bittersweet is not very common and unlikely to be eaten in large quantities; black nightshade berries lose their toxicity as they ripen.

There is very little to be done in case of ingestion of the following plants except to repeatedly induce vomiting while diluting the poison with as much water as possible. And of course, get to a doctor!

Lobelia (*Lobelia* spp.) and wild tobacco (*Nicotiana* spp.) have similar poisonous alkaloids (pyridine and nicotine). *Lobelia kalmi,* found mostly in the Kootenays, is an erect, mostly unbranched plant with an acrid milky juice, alternate lance-shaped leaves and bluish flowers in racemes. It has a two-lipped corolla and five stamens. *Nicotiana attenata* is found in sandy soil east of the Cascades, from Lytton southward. These two plants are not as dangerous as water hemlock.

Baneberry

Actaea spp. Ranunculaceae

Baneberry is a member of the buttercup family. It grows across BC in moist, shady ground and first flowers in April. It has coarse-toothed, thin leaves that are divided in threes two to three times. Leaflets are one to three inches long. Small white flowers form dense clusters with many protruding stamens. Bunches of scarlet or white, glossy, oval berries at the ends of long stalks appear by June or July. Baneberry grows to three feet.

All parts of the plant, but mostly the roots and berries, contain a poisonous glycoside that causes acute stomach cramps, headache, increased pulse, vomiting, delirium, dizziness, circulatory failure, etc. A half-dozen berries can cause symptoms that persist for hours.

Illustration next page

INWOOD '72

Baneberry

Bitter nightshade or bittersweet nightshade
Solanum dulcamara   Solanaceae

Bitter nightshade is one of several poisonous members of the nightshade family, but it is seldom eaten in sufficient amounts to be fatal. It is a climbing or scrambling vine with branches several feet long; the base is often woody. Upper leaves are ovate, and lower leaves are often three-lobed. The wheel-shaped flowers are in panicles opposite a leaf stalk. The corolla is blue to purple with yellow anthers. Flowers and berries can be on the same plant simultaneously from June onward. This plant is well established in moist places near Hope, Osoyoos and Horsefly, and in the Cariboo.

Bittersweet nightshade

Black nightshade
Solanum americanum or *nigrum*   Solanaceae

Black nightshade is a bushy, erect annual shrub found on the southern half of Vancouver Island and in dry places east of the Cascades. It can be found in either sandy or loamy soil and in fields, waste places and open areas. Its leaves are lance-shaped or broader, smooth or slightly lobed. Older leaves are often toothed. Flowers are white and wheel-shaped. Each of the three to eight flowers is about a quarter of an inch across. First flowering is in June, and the growing stem keeps producing new flowers. The berries are first green but become black as they age.

All parts of black nightshade contain the alkaloid solanine, which causes stomach pain, shock, paralysis, diarrhea, vomiting, loss of sensation and dilated pupils. Small amounts can be deadly. The highest concentrations are in the unripe fruit.

Green potatoes and potato sprouts (*Solanum tuberosum*) also contain dangerous amounts of solanine.

The leaves of the common tomato (*Lycopersicon esculentum*) contain a similar poisonous alkaloid.

Broom or scotch broom
Cytisus scoparius   Fabaceae

Broom is a bushy shrub up to six or more feet high, with smooth stems and greenish branches. (The way the long, slender, tough yet flexible branches grow together makes them suitable for brooms—hence the plant's name.) Leaves are alternate, with the lower ones on a short stalk and divided into three small oval leaflets; the upper leaves are stalkless and often reduced to a single leaflet near the branch tips. Bright yellow pea-like flowers are abundant and come one to three to an axil. They are showiest in May and June and last into July. By then, most bushes are thick with small hairy seed pods. Broom is most common on the Gulf Islands and Vancouver Island, where it forms a spring carnival of yellow along the highway from Victoria to north of Campbell River. It appears sporadically in the Interior.

Although herbalists highly recommend broom for kidney and bladder complaints, it causes, in large doses, vomiting and purging, as well as weakening the heart, depressing nerve cells and lowering blood pressure.

Used externally in an ointment, broom is reportedly excellent as a remedy for lice and vermin.

Gorse (*Ulex europaeus*) can be mistaken for broom because of its bushy green form, yellow flowers and similar range. Gorse usually flowers earlier, however, and is a low and sprawling shrub with sharp-pointed needle leaves.

Some lupines (*Lupinus* spp.) contain the same toxic alkaloid found in broom—quinolizidine. The danger is mainly in the seeds.

Death camas
Zigadenus spp.   Melanthiaceae

Death camas has long, flat, grass-like leaves that have a deep groove forming a keel on the opposite side. Flowers are creamy-greenish or yellow-white and have three sepals and three petals, which actually appear to be six petals. Flowers are less than half an inch across. Death camas has an unbranched stem with the leaves usually on the lower part. It is a perennial with a dark-coated bulb shaped like an onion; when not in flower, it can be mistaken for camas or nodding onion. It may be distinguished from nodding onion by the absence of any onion fragrance. It is about 10 to 24 inches high and in flower by mid-April on the coast and early May in the Interior. Two species (*Z. venenosus* and *Z. paniculatus*) are common wherever snow lily, nodding onion or camas grow in BC; one species (*Z. elegans*) is common in alpine meadows.

Alkaloids such as zygadenine are mainly concentrated in the bulb of death camas and cause muscular weakness, subnormal temperature, stomach upset and pain, vomiting, diarrhea and excessive salivation. Zygadenine can be fatal in small quantities.

The underground stem of iris (*Iris* spp.), a close relative of death camas, contains irisin, a violent emetic and cathartic, but this is unlikely to be eaten in quantity because it has a very disagreeable flavour.

Death
camas

Delphinium or larkspur
Delphinium spp.   Ranunculaceae

Eight common species of delphinium are found in BC. They grow from low valleys to alpine heights and flower from the end of April. Leaves are finely and palmately divided and are on long stalks. They are often three inches across. The stem is unbranched and two to four feet high. Flowers are in several shades of light blue and purple, and have five petal-like sepals, one of which is spurred.

The alkaloids delphinine, delphineidin, ajacine and others are found mostly in the seeds and young plants; these cause stomach upset, general weakening, nervous conditions and depression. They are fatal in large quantities. Most of the toxicity is lost after blooming.

Related plants that can cause similar poisoning—also members of the buttercup family—are windflower (*Anemone* spp.) and buttercup (*Ranunculus* spp.). The alkaloid protoanemonin in these plants is highly volatile, and many First Nations groups ate species of buttercup after boiling it to remove the acrid principle.

INWOOD

Delphinium

False hellebore
Veratrum viride and *eschscholtzii*　　　　　　　　Melanthiaceae

False hellebore grows from sea level to alpine elevations in moist areas throughout BC. It has a large unbranched stem (often an inch thick at the base) with many large, heavily ribbed leaves having coarse parallel veins. Leaves can be a foot long and the plant itself three to five feet tall. Flowers are inconspicuous, greenish-white, a half inch across and in thin branching spikes.

False hellebore contains several alkaloids, such as veratrin, that cause salivation, vomiting, diarrhea, stomach pain, paralysis and spasms. It can be fatal in large quantities. The root has been used to slow heartbeat and lower blood pressure, and the gum has been used as a poultice for sprains and rashes. Toxicity decreases as the plant matures.

False hellebore is used as an insect poison.

Foxglove
Digitalis purpurea   Plantaginaceae

Foxglove is a common coastal plant recognized by its spikes of beautiful light-purple-to-white drooping flowers, which are shaped like the fingers of a glove. The flowers, which have dark spots on the lower lip and long hairs inside, bloom in June and July along roadsides and in open fields. Stems grow to three or four feet. The hairy leaves are a foot or more long with sloping lateral veins and slightly indented margins.

Foxglove is commercially cultivated for its digitalin and digitoxin, both used in heart medications. These increase the activity of all forms of muscle tissue, especially the heart and arteries. Large doses can cause cerebral hallucinations and may injure the heart permanently.

Monkshood
Aconitum spp.   Ranunculaceae

Monkshood has alternate, deeply lobed, palmately-veined leaves. The lower leaves have long stems decreasing in length with height. Dark blue flowers grow in long clusters with the upper part hood-like. They are about an inch long and hang from the tip of the main stem or on short side branches. The main stem is sticky and hairy and can be as much as five feet tall. Monkshood is a perennial of rich woods, slopes, mountain creeks and wet meadows. It is found at middle (2,500 feet) to alpine elevations, and it flowers in August. *Aconitum columbianum* is abundant in the mountains around Kootenay Lake and in the Columbia River Valley, and *Aconitum delphinifolium* is common in northern BC and near Hope and Princeton, and in Manning Park.

All parts of monkshood, especially the seeds and roots, contain the alkaloid aconitine, which causes vomiting, diarrhea, spasms, weak pulse, paralysis and convulsions leading to death if taken in quantity. The leaves are most toxic just before flowering.

Monkshood resembles the delphinium genus, but delphiniums have one sepal forming a distinct tapering spur instead of a hood.

INWOOD♀ '72

Monkshood

Pacific bleeding heart
Dicentra formosa and *Dicentra uniflora* Papaveraceae

Bleeding heart has delicately fringed leaves and little or no stem. The leaves nearly hide the flowers, which resemble upside-down steer's heads and have petals that are held together near their tip. Dicentra has a faint, fragrant perfume and shiny black seeds. There are two main species in BC: *Dicentra formosa* is found west of the Cascades and has reddish flowers; *Dicentra uniflora* is found in the wet Interior and has one to two pinkish flowers. Both are found in rich, shady woods to middle mountain elevations and are in flower by early May.

Dicentra is a small plant and unpalatable. All plant parts contain the alkaloid protopine, which causes trembling, staggering, convulsions and laboured breathing.

Bleeding heart

Pacific yew
Taxus brevifolia   Taxaceae

The yew is a small evergreen tree with flat, sharp-pointed needles about an inch long, opposite on the stem, at right angles
and lying flat in the same plane as the stem. The needles are
silver-green underneath. Male and female flowers are on separate trees, and the berries change from green to red around
September. Yew is found in deep shade and in moist flats along
streams. It is a low-altitude tree on Vancouver Island and in
coastal forests and may be found at up to 4,000 feet in the
wet Interior.

All parts of the yew, except for the berry pulp, contain the
alkaloid taxine. This alkaloid causes diarrhea, vomiting, trembling, pupil dilation, breathing difficulties, muscular weakness, collapse, coma, convulsions and slow heartbeat, and it
is fatal in quantity. The leaves are especially poisonous to livestock when cut and piled and allowed to rot.

Poison hemlock
Conium maculatum   Apiacea

Poison hemlock grows on dry ground and in waste places chiefly around Victoria and south of Vancouver. Its leaves are fringed and fern-like and much more finely divided than those of water hemlock. Leaf veins terminate at the tips of the teeth on the leaf margins and not at the notches. Poison hemlock has a hollow stem that is usually purple-spotted, and clusters of small white flowers usually appear by mid-June. The plant grows to a height of four to five feet.

Coniine and other alkaloids are the poisonous elements; the greatest concentration is found in the seeds and roots. Ingestion can cause vomiting, diarrhea, trembling, weak pulse, convulsions, coma and possibly death. Poison hemlock can be mistaken for parsley, but the taste is unpleasant and toxic quantities are seldom consumed.

Poison ivy
Toxicodendron radicans   Anacardiaceae

Poison ivy is found in stony places, rockslides, roadsides and woods. It is not reported west of the Cascades but is common enough in the Interior. A few definite locations are around Quesnel, Seton Lake, Cranbrook, Princeton and the southern Kootenay Valley. Poison ivy leaves are large, wavy-edged and in threes. The middle leaflet has the longest stalk. The leaves are purplish-red in spring and a glossy green in summer. The flowers are small, whitish-green and clustered in the leaf axils. Flowers appear in June but are sometimes absent. The stem may be upright but can trail along the ground. Dull white berries in close clusters partway up the stem appear about mid-July. The plant turns scarlet during the fall and loses its leaves, but the berries may remain all winter. Winter buds are brown, woolly and without scales.

Skin irritation is caused by the oil pentadecylcatechol, which is present in all parts of the shrub. Washing as soon as possible with much soapy water helps remove the irritant oil. Epsom salts, calamine lotion or infusions of gumweed, chickweed or sorrel can provide relief. A good soap can be made by mixing ashes and animal grease.

Poison oak is relatively rare in BC. It is occasionally found on the Gulf Islands, on southern Vancouver Island and near the lower Fraser River. Like poison ivy, it can be a shrub or a climber, has glossy leaves in threes and bears white berries in the fall.

Spreading dogbane
Apocynum spp.

Apocynaceae

Dogbane is a common plant in BC, growing in either dry and exposed or moist and shady soils. It is found from sea level to 3,000 feet on the coast and to 5,500 feet in the Interior. Leaves are opposite, thick, egg-shaped and sharp-pointed, and they hang down in the heat. Flowers are white to rose, and green in *Apocynum cannabinum* (Indian hemp). The stem is smooth and reddish and breaks to reveal a sticky, milky juice. Dogbane has long, curved "string bean" seed pods that are three to five inches long. Each silky seed bears a tuft of hairs. The plant is a perennial, often growing to five feet. Flowers have five sepals and five petals, and appear in May or June.

Dogbane root contains a powerful heart stimulant similar in action to digitalis. In small amounts, it is a tonic. The root is officially used for Bright's disease and heart irregularities. It is also used for fever, poor digestion, gallstones, diabetes, rheumatism, dysfunction of the liver and kidneys, and stiff joints. But with so many safer herbs available, it is better not to experiment with this plant. The juice from the stem is known to be poisonous to livestock, although no cases of human poisoning have been recorded.

Dogbane seeds can be eaten after being parched or ground into meal. First Nations used the juice as a hair tonic and buckskin cleanser. Ropes and nets can be made from both stem and root fibre.

Illustration next page

Dogbane

Water hemlock
Cicuta maculata or *douglasii*   Apiaceae

Water hemlock is common only in marshes, brackish ponds and moist habitats. It has long, finely toothed, pinnately compound leaves. Side branchlets often branch again into short stems holding three leaflets. Small white flowers cluster in rounded heads. When cut open, the thick underground portion of the stem reveals horizontal chambers. The plant is usually about six feet tall. Leaf veins terminate mostly at the notches and not at the teeth tips. Leaf stalks are smooth and hairless, and yellow juice exudes when stem or root is cut. Water hemlock flowers from mid-June onwards.

The poisons, found mostly in the rootstalk, cause diarrhea, violent convulsions, spasms, tremors, extreme stomach pain, frothing at the mouth, delirium and death. One mouthful can be fatal.

Illustration next page

Water hemlock

Other potentially dangerous plants in BC include wild pea (*Lathyrus* spp.), some of which have poisonous seeds; rhubarb, which has poisonous leaves and often escapes cultivation; snowberry (*Symphoricarpos albus*), whose leaves contain saponin; ragwort (*Senecio* spp.), containing an alkaloid that causes liver damage; and laurels, azaleas and rhododendrons (*Kalmia* and *Rhododendron* spp.), which, like Labrador tea, contain andromedotoxin.

Appendix

SOME FOOD USES

BOILED: Arrowhead root, salsify root, spring beauty bulb, thistle root, balsamroot, camas, burdock root and onions.

CANDIED: ginger root, rose petals and violets.

AS A COOL DRINK: elderberries, pipsissewa root and leaves, sorrel leaves, camomile, mint, mallow and chickweed.

GROUND FOR FLOUR OR MUSH: lamb's quarters seeds, plantain seeds, shepherd's purse seeds, balsamroot seeds, root and seeds of biscuitroot, prickly pear cactus seeds, pine nuts and hazelnuts.

AS AN HERB BEER: camomile flowers, dandelion leaves and nettle leaves.

AS A HOT TEA: alfalfa leaves, camomile, clover, elderflowers, fireweed, ginger, goldenrod, sarsaparilla, snowbrush, mint, rose petals and hips, yarrow, sage, biscuitroot leaves and flowers, berry flowers and leaves, conifer shoots, juniper berries, Labrador tea, ground ivy and parsley.

FOR IRON: chickweed, garlic, purslane, parsley, seaweeds and nettles.

PICKLED: glasswort and purslane.

AS A POT-HERB OR IN SOUPS: any of the above plus young burdock leaves, clover flowers, young comfrey leaves, horsetail shoots, nettle leaves, onion bulbs and flowers, salsify leaves and root, elderberries, ginger root, balsamroot leaves and root, root of biscuitroot, bitterroot, monkey flowers, young coltsfoot leaves, young mustard leaves and arrowhead tubers.

RAW OR IN SALADS: chopped or powdered alfalfa leaves, cattail shoots, young chicory leaves, young dandelion leaves and crown, young fireweed leaves and buds, lamb's quarters leaves, plantain leaves, young false Solomon's seal leaves, rosehips, spring beauty leaves and flowers, stonecrop leaves, watercress leaves and flowers, biscuitroot leaves and flowers, prickly pear cactus leaves and fruit, chickweed leaves and flowers, glasswort, miner's lettuce leaves and flowers, purslane leaves and flowers, strawberry blite berries, sunflower seeds, parsley, chopped or powdered seaweeds, berries, bulrush shoots, bur reed shoots and orach.

ROASTED: Arrowhead root, salsify root, spring beauty bulb, thistle root and seeds, balsamroot, biscuitroot, camas, sunflower seeds, hazelnuts, burdock root and onions.

ROASTED AND GROUND AS COFFEE: burdock root, chicory root, dandelion root and sunflower seeds.

AS A SALT: monkey flowers, coltsfoot and seaweeds.

AS A SEASONING: juniper berries, seaweeds, glasswort, sage, mustard, garlic, biscuitroot leaves and parsley.

AS A SYRUP: cherries, prickly pear cactus leaves and fruit, camas bulbs, berries, poplar sap, birch sap, rosehips, mint, ginger root and violets.

FOR VITAMIN A: alfalfa, lamb's quarters, shepherd's purse, dandelion, chicory, onion, nettles, curled dock, watercress, mustards, garlic, purslane and parsley.

FOR VITAMIN B: garlic, mustards and sunflower seeds.

FOR VITAMIN C: elderberries, rosehips, nettles, shepherd's purse, dock, kinnikinnick, pipsissewa, chicory, dandelion, watercress, sorrel, mustards, garlic, purslane, parsley and conifer needles.

FOR VITAMIN D: alfalfa, nettles and watercress.

FOR VITAMIN E: watercress, parsley, nettles, dandelion and alfalfa.

AS WINE: dandelion flowers, cherries, elderberries and other berries.

SOME MEDICINAL USES

ATHLETE'S FOOT: clover flowers and the juice of onion or garlic.

BRONCHIAL AND LUNG DISORDERS: chickweed, garlic, coltsfoot (Tussilago), sage, pine, mustard, Labrador tea, comfrey, ginger, mullein, violet and clover.

COLIC: camomile, mint and horehound.

COLON AILMENTS: mallow, fireweed, ginger root and dandelion leaves.

CONTRACEPTION: juniper berries, dogbane root, ginger root, milkweed root and false Solomon's seal.

COUGHING: cherry bark, garlic, gumweed, mallow, sage, milkweed, coltsfoot (Tussilago), Labrador tea, alfalfa flowers, clover flowers, comfrey, mint, mullein, skullcap leaves and valerian root.

CROTCH ITCH: nettle and chickweed.

DIARRHEA: prickly pear cactus, blackberry roots, cherry bark, wild strawberry, alum root, cinquefoil root, comfrey, elderberries, ginger, shepherd's purse, yarrow, fireweed and stonecrop.

DRY SKIN: elderflowers, yarrow and violet.

EARACHE: warmed oil from garlic or onion.

EXPELLING AFTERBIRTH: skullcap, chokecherry gum and mallow root.

FEVER: milkweed, juniper berries, willow inner bark, sarsaparilla root, shepherd's purse, sorrel, dock, violet, yarrow and thistle root.

HEADACHE: balsamroot, willow bark, cherry bark, parsley, mint, garlic, violet, skullcap, cinquefoil root and valerian.

HICCUPING: mint, elderflowers, skullcap leaves and yarrow leaves.

TO INCREASE BREASTMILK AND FOR SORE BREASTS: poultice or tea of milkweed, parsley, woodruff, comfrey or St. John's wort.

INCREASING MENSTRUATION: parsley, St. John's wort, ginger root, yarrow, nettle and valerian.

INDIGESTION: camomile, ginger, mint, garlic, gumweed, purslane and sage.

INSECT STING: camomile, comfrey, nettle seeds, plantain, sorrel, dock, balsamroot, garlic, mallow, juniper berries, parsley and Labrador tea.

INTERNAL PURIFICATION: garlic, onion, sage, parsley, elderflowers, nettle leaves, Oregon grape root, sarsaparilla root, alfalfa, dandelion, ginger root, kinnikinnick, shepherd's purse, yarrow, and pipsissewa.

INTERNAL ULCERS: raspberry leaves, chickweed, garlic, mallow, cinquefoil root, comfrey, horsetail shoots and mullein.

IRRITATED MUCOUS MEMBRANES: chickweed, garlic, mallow, fireweed, Oregon grape root, yarrow and lamb's quarters.

JOINT ACHES AND PAINS: broomrape, sage, willow bark, parsley, mustard, birch sap, cinquefoil root, comfrey and fireweed.

KIDNEY AND BLADDER AILMENTS: chicory root, kinnikinnick leaves, dandelion leaves, pipsissewa leaves, plantain leaves, sorrel leaves, horsetail shoots, dock leaves, broomrape, mallow, parsley, juniper berries, broom and birch sap.

LICE: broomrape, delphinium, Labrador tea and broom.

LIVER AILMENTS: gumweed, purslane, chicory root, dandelion leaves and snowbrush leaves.

MENSTRUAL PAIN: mullein, yarrow, ginger root, camomile, comfrey, sorrel, valerian, violet and mint.

MENSTRUAL PERIOD TONIC: sage.

NASAL MEMBRANE CONGESTION OR IRRITATION: gumweed, milkweed, sage, wormwood, mustard, juniper berries, spruce, pine, hemlock, fir, Douglas fir, cherry bark, mullein leaves, comfrey, yarrow, clover flowers, ginger root, mint, nettle, onion and garlic.

NAUSEA: mint leaves and horehound.

NERVOUSNESS: garlic, onion, sage, cherry bark, camomile, clover, mint, skullcap and valerian root.

POISON OAK OR IVY: gumweed, chickweed and sorrel.

PURGATIVE: elder bark, false Solomon's seal seeds, camas in quantity and milkweed bark.

RASH: yarrow and elderflowers.

REDUCING BLEEDING: purslane, alder bark, chokecherry juice, cinquefoil root, comfrey, fireweed, yarrow, horsetail, nettle, shepherd's purse, kinnikinnick, alum root and plantain.

RELAXATION BEFORE CHILDBIRTH: juniper berries, cedar and prickly pear cactus.

RHEUMATISM: balsamroot, gumweed, sage, parsley, mustard, juniper berries, birch sap, fireweed, pipsissewa, sarsaparilla root, shepherd's purse and false Solomon's seal root.

RINGWORM: garlic and milkweed.

SKIN DISEASES: garlic, onion, alder bark, birch sap, burdock, dandelion root, pipsissewa leaves and sarsaparilla root.

SORE EYES (AS A WASH): chickweed, mallow, camomile, elderflowers, onion, garlic, violet and sarsaparilla root.

SORE FEET: hemlock leaves and alder leaves.

SORE THROAT OR MOUTH: birch sap, garlic, gumweed, mallow, sage, wormwood, pine buds, Douglas fir buds, fir buds, spruce buds, Labrador tea, elderflowers, ginger root, mint, mullein, violet, yarrow, camomile, comfrey root, clover, sarsaparilla root and horehound.

STAPH INFECTION: garlic and devil's club root.

TEETHING PAIN: mallow, sage, wormwood, mint and skullcap.

TONIC AFTER CHILDBIRTH: sage and St. John's wort.

TOOTHACHE: garlic, onion, gumweed, sage, camomile, mullein and yarrow.

VAGINAL DISCHARGE: douche or tea of Oregon grape root, violet leaves, yarrow, juniper berries and kinnikinnick.

WARTS AND CORNS: dandelion juice, mullein oil and root, and milkweed.

WORMS: garlic, onion, sage, horehound and nettle.

WOUNDS, BURNS, INFLAMMATION AND BRUISES: seaweeds, alder, willow, poplar, conifer shoots, mallow, sage, chickweed, garlic, gumweed, milkweed, St. John's wort, camomile, comfrey, elder, nettle, Oregon grape bark, shepherd's purse, plantain, stonecrop, violet, false Solomon's seal and alum root.

SOME OTHER USES

AS A DYE: prickly pear cactus, alder, sage, sunflower, hemlock, camomile, goldenrod, nettle root and Oregon grape root and bark.

AS FIBRE OR MATERIAL: nettle stalk, plantain leaves, cattail shoots, milkweed, grasses, cedar bark, willow shoots, spreading dogbane, bulrush and bur reed.

AS AN INSECT REPELLENT: sage oil, garlic oil, false hellebore, vanilla leaf, woodruff, Labrador tea, camomile, elder, nettle and onion.

IN SAUNA STEAM: sage, yarrow, camomile, mints, elderflowers, goldenrod and mullein.

AS A SCENT: vanilla leaf, woodruff, rose petals, violet flowers, elderflowers, snowbrush flowers, conifer needles, camomile, clover, mints and yarrow.

SHAMPOO AND HAIR RINSE: camomile flowers, nettle, yarrow flowers, snowbrush flowers and sage.

AS SOAP: snowbrush flowers and sunflower oil.

AS A SOOTHING BATH: chickweed, sage, mustards, conifer needles, camomile, valerian, clover, mints, elderflowers, goldenrod flowers and woodruff.

TOOTH CLEANSER: sage and wormwood.

Index of Plants

Illustrations are indicated in **bold**.